Golf Beats Us All

GOLF

BEATS US ALL

(And So We Love It)

Joseph A. Amato

Johnson Books

BOULDER

Published in the United States by Johnson Books, a division of Johnson Publishing Company, 1880 South 57th Court, Boulder, Colorado 80301.

9 8 7 6 5 4 3 2 1

Library of Congress Cataloging-in-Publication Data
Amato, Joseph Anthony.
  Golf beats us all (and so we love it) / Joseph A. Amato.
    p. cm.
  Includes index.
  ISBN 1-55566-192-0 (pbk.: alk. paper)
  1. Golf—Philosophy. 2. Golf—Psychological aspects. I. Title.
GV967.A49 1997   97-3911
796.352'01—dc21   CIP

Printed in the United States by
Johnson Printing
1880 South 57th Court
Boulder, Colorado 80301

♻ Printed on recycled paper with soy ink

To Don Olsen—

Librarian, printer, poet,
friend & golfer

CONTENTS

FOREWORD

JOE AMATO AND I got started in our love affair with golf the same way—that is, as bag rats or loopies, commonly called caddies.

We saw it all—from the once-a-year player who would make several shots that made no noise, to the finely-tuned competitive amateurs, and of course, the touring pros. Although their swings and thought processes were miles apart, they all experienced, as Joe points out, the longest distance in golf—from the practice tee to the first tee.

He describes the solitude of golf and the never-ending imagination of golf shots that we all have. Your mind will have flashbacks to shots that you first imagined and then hit. Some of these were successful, some not. But success is sometimes easier to remember and certainly more fun.

My flashback is to 1984. In the finals of our member-guest invitational, my partner and I found ourselves in a sudden-death playoff for the championship. You won't need a caddie for this story because it lasts only one hole.

Faced with a 218-yard second shot to a 500-yard par five, I thought to myself—go out in style, hit the knife. If I failed, everyone would agree that the shot was too tough, as no one can hit a 1-iron, but if I succeeded, the story would be locked in a corner of my mind forever.

The ball looked as big as a baseball, with the late afternoon sun at our backs. The scores of people watching were dressed in their finery for the celebration dinner dance.

It worked! Safely on in two with two putts from 35 feet did the job. The thoughts of a local football coach, Al Fracassa, came to mind. He always told his kids, "If you can conceive it, and you believe it, you can achieve it." This is in keeping with what Joe alludes to in Chapter Three, Delights and Ecstasies.

Joe Amato explores some of the oddities of this game. How do you define the perfect swing? Why did early players score so well with just a few clubs?

Chick Evans won the U.S. Open in 1916 with seven clubs by shooting a 286 at Minikada Country Club in Minneapolis. That score remained a record until 1936 when Tony Manero shot 282 to set a new U.S. Open standard.

Players with just a few clubs were great shotmakers—they had to be. However, in the 1930s, and until the USGA declared a limit of 14 clubs in 1938, many players went the other direction and carried 25 to 35 clubs.

They even had half graduations in their irons, such as 6, 6½, 7, 7½, 8, and so forth. One of the must ludicrous and humorous stories involved an extremely capable player named Clarence Gomber. After a particularly finessed shot to one hole, a fellow competitor asked what club he had hit. Clarence answered, "I hit a three-quarter 7½ iron."

The naming of clubs that Joe refers to is universal. All the colorful people name at least one of their clubs, and many people of average demeanor may have very colorful names for various clubs. Some people were even named after clubs, such as a guy at Baldwin Hills in California named 3-Iron Jones because that is what he hit off the tee on nearly every hole. He of course whetted a piece of grass for the face to reduce any chance of reverse spin that would shorten his drive.

There is much reflective thought running as a continuous thread throughout *Golf Beats Us All.* There is no one answer to this game. What works for you might not, and most probably will not, work for your regular Saturday morning partner. We are all eternal searchers trying to find the answer, whether it be a swing thought or a strategy thought.

Joe explores the fun and the folly of this wonderful game. He talks about hitting the shots we fear, and that generally produce failure. He talks of choking, which we all do, in golf and in everyday life.

But he also adds that defeat is so necessary from time to time. We have to put things into perspective, and failure in golf is so often a restarting point. We have to remember that an airplane has to turn into the wind to take off.

Have fun with *Golf Beats Us All.* I did.

Robert L. McMasters
President, Western Golf Association
(and former Bag Rat)

PREFACE

I HAVE LONG BEEN FASCINATED by the myriad of pleasures offered by golf. And like any player, I remain intrigued by the fact that golfers find such pleasure in a game that causes so much pain, wastes so much time, and whose outcome is of utter insignificance.

Probably for the same reason that I like the challenge of playing golf when the wind is up and the course is tough, I am predisposed to reflecting on the inner side of golf. I was also attracted to the idea that if I understood something about the pleasures of golf, I would also understand something about human experience.

Golf's pleasures are many, as they are not easily inventoried and they are even less easily explored and defined. Yet they offer the full horizon of human pleasures. To learn about the game's pleasures is a road to self-knowledge.

We say we play golf for pleasure, but few of us care to consider what this means. We are seldom as honest as an old bachelor member at my home course in rural Minnesota. He confesses to liking golf because it gives him a good excuse to talk to himself. He once said, "Without a wife and lawn, I need golf. What else is there to pick at!"

Indeed, the great majority of us—at least most of the time—would rather risk breaking our necks on the slippery clubhouse floor than be caught by some sort of "low draw-hook Socrates" who would interrogate us about our supposed pleasure derived from golf. Better to risk our necks than to have our heads turned to mash by critical self-examination.

However, I must confess—indeed, this book is my confession—that at least once I failed to escape a "low draw-hook Socrates." He injected me with his venomous questioning. Since that day—whenever and wherever it was—I confess suffering periods of feverish questioning about golf's pleasures. In my worst deliriums, I even believed I could outthink the game that I could never outplay.

Perhaps I was destined to a lifetime of reflection on the game, which I have known since I started to caddie as a boy of twelve. How could this game, which so throws you back upon yourself, not occupy a mind shaped by the Catholic confessional (the curtained workshop of self-examination of pleasure and intention) and trained as a philosopher and historian? I further confess that I have always had a turn towards flushing out the inner meaning of things. In the course of writing this book, I did what is surely too fashionable these days: I added a therapeutic goal to my efforts. I insisted that the injunction "Know thyself!" included the command, "Name and examine thy pleasures." In any case, a person who won't acknowledge his pleasures is not likely to have or be a good time. And he or she surely won't arrive at the wisdom of our club's old bachelor, who starts off every round on the first tee by saying to himself, "Aim 'em, hit 'em, and let 'em fly."

I do hope that this book will help my fellow golfers to better know themselves and their games. Of course, I do not promise to improve their play, unless self-knowledge is worth (as I believe it to be) a stroke or two a nine. I also intend to satisfy the philosopher who secretly lurks in every golfer. We have all been bitten (admittedly or not) by some kind of golf Socrates.

I begin and end the book with autobiographical and historical material. The book begins when I was a young caddie, aspiring to be a professional, at the Country Club of Detroit in the early 1950s. I conclude with a return visit to the country club where I caddied forty years earlier. I use the Introduction to examine my first love of the game, which underpins my understanding of the game's pleasures, ecstasies, and wisdom. In the Conclusion, I reflect on the history of the game since I was a boy.

Following the autobiographical Introduction, Chapter One attempts to define the horizon of golf's pleasures. And from there the reader can proceed to follow an increasing refinement of the subject of pleasure as I pursue the subjects of ecstasy, grace, pain, character, and wisdom. Along the way, I hope the reader will pick up threads that lead toward the center of human experience, and I hope by the Conclusion that he will have defined his own golfing pleasures. Finally, I confess that I will be disappointed if the reader of *Golf Beats Us All* hasn't picked up a few useful tips and a handful of anecdotes and stories he believes to be worthy of repetition.

ACKNOWLEDGMENTS

EVERY BOOK I HAVE WRITTEN has been a matter of considerable gratitude. And each time I write acknowledgments, I am filled with a feeling of strong guilt (a kind of anticipated remorse) that comes from the sense of near certainty that I have forgotten someone who deserves to be thanked. The writing of these acknowledgments proves no exception. In fact, as I write them, I think of how missed short putts spoil our best-played holes.

So in writing the acknowledgments to *Golf Beats Us All* I take the advice of golf immortal Harry Vardon concerning the many short putts he missed. "Miss them quick!" Vardon said. I finish these acknowledgments, saying quickly but earnestly, thank all of you who have somehow helped along the way but I may have forgotten. Equally hastily, I confess, all misses are my own.

Beyond that, I simply make a chronological list of those who directly helped me at important points as this book went from notes (written with the worst writing instrument of all, golf course pencils) on scraps of paper and scorecards, collected at the bottom of the ball pocket of my bag to the publication of this full-length book.

Five years ago, I was having a conversation with Galen Skramstad, the best of the many good local golfers. Galen (who reads about, as well as plays, the game) asked why I didn't write a book about golf. Clinching his argument (at least this is my recollection), Galen said: "You seem to write about everything else!"

He didn't realize he was throwing me into the briar patch of my own desires, as he was saying aloud what had already crossed my mind more than once. In fact, in one of my cabinets, I already had a dozen or so notes on a golf book. And more than that, he had just invited me to what compulsive writers do: they insist on turning the possibility of a book into the reality of a book. They can't bury the thing until it is laid to rest in type.

I was drawn to the task of trying to get to the bottom of explaining the game that had brought so much and so many different pleasures to me in my forties and fifties. At another level I was trying to understand a first love. I was attracted to the idea of trying, as an adult, to beat on paper the game that had beaten me on the grass, however much I had loved it as an earnest young boy.

Soon after my conversations with Galen, my solitary rounds of golf—which have recently won me the nickname "Back Nine Joe" from Allen Lucht, the local professional—were interrupted by notetaking. For a short period, the very first thing I did before going to the course was to make sure that my bag contained a pencil and notepad. So golf seasons passed, many rounds were played, notes were taken which in turn were transformed into short essays and outlines, and now this book.

Three close friends helped me with the book. My friend David Monge (a minister and theologian, but not much of a golfer) encouraged me greatly when he declared that he saw in an early draft of the manuscript a good work in the making. His remark came at a time when I needed encouragement as I struggled mightily to carve a book out of pleasures, pains, and wisdom. Between its autobiographical beginnings and the

critical historical conclusion, I equally fought both the golfer
and philosopher in me to achieve the proper mix of ideas and
details, insights and stories. I was also delighted when he recognized that below the surface of the text I had carried on a
commentary on grace.

Don Olsen also kept the manuscript alive for me when he
praised it as potentially "a golf classic." A long-time friend,
poet, librarian, and fine golfer who was player-captain of the
University of Minnesota's golf team in the 1950s, Don knows
the game inside and out as well as anyone I know. In two
lengthy and well-written letters, Don accompanied his criti-
cisms of the manuscript with many telling anecdotes and personal stories that have been incorporated into the book. For
them, his enthusiasm, and in memory of the rounds we
played together, I dedicate this book to him.

Scott Perrizo of Crossings Press—friend, writer, pigeon
raiser, and golf aficionado himself—gave this manuscript its
final edit, then designed and produced the book's pages. His
touch was fine. Once again he improved my work. He instantly established a kinship with the manuscript and never
ceased caring about it until it was printed.

Scott did one more thing for the manuscript. He praised it
to his wife, Mira, who is Managing Editor at Johnson Books.
She in turn recommended it to her colleagues: Barbara Mussil,
Publisher; Stephen Topping, Editorial Director; and Richard
Croog, Sales and Promotion Director. They accepted it,
found a title for it, and promoted it. For that, I am thankful to
the nice folks at Johnson Books.

Three other people helped the book along. Robert McMasters, player and captain of the University of Michigan golf
team in the 1950s, University of Michigan Evans Scholar, and
present President of Western Golf, wrote a Foreword to the
work. Leon Rappoport, friend of spirit and Kansas State

University psychologist, wrote an Afterword for non-golfers who are interested in the inner side of golf. Joseph Murdoch, life-time golf bibliophile, historian, golf collector, and founder of the Golf Collectors' Society, offered praise of the book and has done much to make sure that the book, most important of all, gets read.

Finally, I wish to thank my daughter, Beth, my son, Adam, and my wife, Catherine. Memories of Beth's natural swing and outstanding high school play reminded me of how many of golf's skills are natural gifts. Adam, a fellow golfer who has battled me even for the last ten years, frequently asked about the book, offered some of his ideas, and listened to me describe the book's fate. My wife, Catherine, has graced my life and tolerated my three great as possible obsessions: writing, history, and golf. It is not easy to relax around someone like me who, even when he purportedly sits down to watch television, continually jumps up to read a passage, check a footnote, or test his putting stroke. But the truth is, not unlike me, she sits little and jumps up as well. In an age of watching, we prefer doing.

And, this brings me to my final wish and advice for the reader of this book: I hope that after sitting and reading *Golf Beats Us All,* you jump up and enjoy and understand golf. The game is yours to enjoy, even if it beats you now and then, and again.

"But such a day tomorrow as today,
And to be boy eternal."
—*William Shakespeare,* **The Winter's Tale**

INTRODUCTION

Loops & Rounds

W<small>HEN</small> I <small>WAS A BOY</small>, I was never happier than when I would set out, with a bag of rattling clubs on my shoulder, for the nearby municipal golf course. On the course I was on my own. There I belonged to a group of boys. Each had his own swing and a little money to bet. We challenged adults as equals, and we took special pleasure in defeating them. I remember a skins game with two older men when my friend and partner, Ron Helveston, purposely missed a four-footer so I could make a three-footer to win the hole. I did it with a birdie 3. I felt a lot of pride in having hustled the two men—and more pride in not having missed a three-footer.

Chandler Park—a modest municipal course on the east side of Detroit—was my home course, and where we played our high school matches. We knew the course, the small clubhouse, and the holes in the chain-link fence that we could sneak through when we were short of the thirty-five cent greens fee. We knew each hole like the back of our hands. I

1

still remember the hedge-lined first and tenth holes and the 250-yard par-three third. I remember the second hole, where a fellow hit a ball in my bag on the fly and, when he approached me and asked where his ball went, I simply emptied my bag out and his ball fell in front of him. I clearly remember the fourth and ninth holes. In one round, the shots of my friend, Donnie Sam, hit the same guy on each of these two holes.

At Chandler Park I played out the first passion of my life, my desire to be a great golfer. On that humble course, reduced by a few hundred yards in length in the mid-1950s by construction of the crosstown throughway I-94, I confess that I suffered my first adolescent doubts about my ability to command my own future happiness.

I was twelve in the late summer of 1950 when my friend Ron took me to caddie at the Country Club of Detroit in Grosse Pointe Farms. I had no idea of just how exclusive the country club was when I turned off Morross Road ("Seven Mile Road") at the small, old cemetery and followed winding tree-lined Country Club Lane for a few hundred yards. Then I entered the club's large parking lot, over which towered the immense clubhouse, three stories high. Built in the late twenties in the English country home style, the interior (which I was not to see until much later) included galleries, a great hall, high oak-beamed ceilings, and a grill, a restaurant, recreation rooms and a bowling alley in the basement. Its roof was many-gabled and covered by a wonderful black and blue slate, which added solemnity to this place where members ate, drank, played cards, tennis, paddle-tennis, polo, went swimming or ice skated. Its long, elevated, front stone porch looked directly down on the green of the difficult par-four eighteenth. Its molded fairways traversed by bunkers and deep roughs, and its bunker-framed and elevated greens made me feel I had come to work in a magic garden. So much grass, so much care, such an elaborate place to play—at first glance the course defined for me (a boy from the working classes) the meaning of wealth.

Before I went to the country club to caddie, I knew that Grosse Pointe Farms was where the rich, "the really rich," people of Detroit lived. Our family had taken many Sunday drives from our home at Harper and McNichols (a new working- and middle-class neighborhood) out to Lake St. Clair. We would follow Jefferson Avenue out for approximately three miles to see the great estates with their immense lawns and servants' quarters along the lake. As a matter of ritual, we passed each with an "ooh" and an "ah." Each mansion seemed even greater and more opulent than the preceding one. The lives of the people who lived in these mansions exceeded our imaginations. Having passed the beautiful yacht club, also built in the twenties, we would finish our tour at the long stone wall of Ford's estate, where the only entry was a roadway that passed beneath a large servants' gatehouse. Because this was Ford's mansion and it was invisible from the road, we assumed it must be the greatest mansion of all.

This beautiful area on Lake St. Clair had grown up to serve the expanding pleasures of Detroit's multiplying industrialists. It belonged originally to the Native Americans and then to French farmers, who worked traditional long, narrow strips of land that went from the lake inland. In the middle of the nineteenth century, it became the site of roadhouses and summer resorts for increasing numbers of the wealthy from the nearby booming industrial city of Detroit. (Detroit's population grew from 9,000 in 1840 to 285,000 in 1900 to 993,000 in 1920.) Detroit's rich, like the rich everywhere in the industrial Western world at that time, sought to escape "the dust and din" they themselves created. They built factories in one place and found their pleasure in another. My father, the child of Sicilian immigrants, came to Detroit at age three. He had a booster's pride for his city that included a detailed knowledge of Detroit's industries, buildings, waterworks, sports teams, and native sons, and his knowledge supplied me with a thorough background of our home.

Originally, the clubhouse was on the lake and the course ran across ribbon-like farms in more or less straight lines away from the lake and back again, like the early Scottish links that led along the ocean and back. The course's layout has a rich and checkered history. It followed the cost of rents, the purchase and sale of real estate, and battles among members advocating different sports. These battles were concluded in 1927 with the building of the present clubhouse and the completion of the golf course.

What I knew first and best about the club was the caddie shack, a low brick building to the right of the first tee. It was joined to the pro shop, which displayed golf equipment and clothing too expensive for me to even covet. Behind it was the club room, which stored four to five hundred bags of clubs. The front room of the caddie shack faced the first tee and belonged to the caddie master. Through the window that connected the two rooms, the caddie master, Caesar Raimondi, called us for loops or occasional scoldings, and we received our pay, or bought pop, potato chips, candies, and the ever-popular, velvety-soft Twinkies.

In the caddie shack and out behind it, we were free, within limits, to do what we wanted. We gambled, talked, and worked on our short game. Only rarely did we fall under the sharp eyes and intimidating tongue of Caesar, who served as caddie master for fifty years before his retirement in 1977. When we didn't get an early morning loop (which commonly happened in the summer to new caddies), we amused ourselves as best we could. Sitting on the long-slotted blond benches, we smoked, caught flies in flight with our hands, pitched pennies, and played cards. Often we went out back and shot baskets, pitched horseshoes, watched members hit balls on the adjacent driving range, went down to the old hole (a remnant of an earlier course) to hit some balls, or hung out under the trees along the side of the range and wise-cracked with fellow caddies.

Caddies were graded B, A, and Master Caddies, a ranking that determined how much we would be paid. B's received, if I recall correctly, $1.75 for eighteen, A's $2.00, and masters $2.25 and the rate was twice as much if you carried doubles. Also, your rank, in combination with Caesar's inscrutable judgment, determined whether you got the members who tipped well, a comparatively rare breed at our club. Guests almost always tipped better than our own members.

Before a caddie could get on the course, he was taught a number of things. Our long instruction list included these rules: Be quiet and stay still; always face the member when he is addressing the ball; replace divots and repair ball marks on the green. A caddie had to be especially sure to loosen the pin before the member struck his shot. He also had to avoid casting his shadow over the golfer's line of play. There were also rules of golf whose infraction by a caddie might cost players two penalty strokes, the loss of a hole, or even disqualification. This added seriousness to the job.

Beyond this, a good caddie also learned other skills. He familiarized himself with each hole. He estimated distances, judged the likely consequences of different types of shots off certain types of lies, grasses, and sands, and read greens. And he had to match this knowledge with an assessment of his player's ability and temperament. Caddies who played the game themselves were more likely to master the higher skills of caddying. However, there was a tendency on their part to make their player play their game.

A caddie needed strength and endurance. Nothing was as hard for us young boys, when, weighing barely more than a hundred and twenty pounds, we carried "doubles," the bags of two long-hitting and long-striding players. Invariably, when we had doubles, one player would hit hooks, while the other hit slices. The heavy leather bags of the period always had a bothersome umbrella attached to the side and were commonly filled with dozens of balls, a coat, sweater, two hats, and whatever else a member happened, over the course of several seasons, to jam into his bag.

Caddies formed a community of their own. At its crudest level, the caddie community was based on who you could beat up in a fight. A pecking order determined that the weakest caddies were "Spooks" and "Spiders." For one season, the caddies were terrorized by Mean Jack, an older, pale blue-eyed, muscular, angry kid. Everyone skirted him. He was rumored to carry a knife. To get better tips, Mean Jack would step on opposing players' balls to insure his own player's victory. Mean Jack once lifted a member, who accused him of stealing balls, off the ground and held him up against a tree and kept him there until the member apologized to Jack for accusing him of what Jack had actually done. Caesar got rid of Mean Jack.

Of course, fights (and the likes of Mean Jack) were exceptions. We all came mainly from the working classes and we all heeded Caesar's call. We did have, as probably every caddie house did back then, two old winos, "Old John" and Al, both in their late forties or early fifties. They frequently celebrated the end of their day's work by finishing off a bottle of Mogen David in the shade of a large tree at the end of the driving range. Later, I was reminded of them in the company of the old Scottish caddies of St. Andrews, whose days ended in the local pub.

As caddies—at least us regulars—we had the pleasure of our own lore. A large part of it was composed of stories about members: how well they played, how much they cheated, bet, or what outrageous things they said or did. A favorite caddie story was how Tom McMahon, hands down the club's longest hitter, won $14,000 from William Clay Ford (a decent golfer himself). McMahon successfully got two of ten second shots on the slightly elevated and trapped green of the newly lengthened 600-yard, par-five tenth. Any mention of betting always brought up club member Fred Kammer, who won the club championship fifteen times (from 1942 to 1969), reached the finals of the National Amateur twice, and also played on the United States Walker Cup Team. Mr. Kammer was rumored among us caddies to bet hundreds of dollars on each stroke over or below par. Once, I remember, he even made his bet at 71, which was a stroke below par.

Frequently, caddies ended their discussion of high-stakes betting by referring to millionaire members who got pleasure out of betting nickels or dimes in a game for first on the green, first down, and lowest score on the hole. (The silly game was appropriately called Bingo-Bango-Bungo.) Caddies, who saw the pots of individual card games reach as high as fifty dollars on long rainy days in the caddie shed, disdained these members' parsimonious Bingo-Bango-Bungo as much as they praised the high-stakes betting of Ford, McMahon, and Kammer.

As pubescent caddies, we loved "the romance story" of our '54 National Amateur. One member's daughter, of truly Marilyn Monroe–like proportions and glamour, set the caddie house on fire during the closing rounds when she strolled down the fairway hand-in-hand with Robert Sweeny, the wealthy, debonair player from England. The two even made one brief stop in the eleventh-hole bathroom during his championship match against Arnold Palmer. Many of us, who were caddie-golfers, were stunned that he could be so close to her and still keep his eye on the ball. Perhaps, I have since thought, she was a stratagem used to disturb the serenity of the young Palmer.

Caddies' favorite stories also involved their relationships to their players. One of our caddies had the distinction of dropping Sam Snead's bag on the second hole and telling the highly critical Snead that he should carry his own bag.

One late Fall day, I was caddying for old Bernie Stroh. Nearly blind, Mr. Stroh looked like he carried one of his brewery's barrels in his protruding stomach. While we were looking for his ball in the deep left rough of the third hole, he mistakenly addressed and, before I could say anything, hit a mushroom. When he asked me where his shot had gone, I was forced to reply, "Sir, you struck a mushroom, sir." He replied, "Oh!" and continued to look for his ball, as if hitting mushrooms was a common part of his golfing experience.

Known as the best tipper at the club, giving as much as two dollars for eighteen holes, I was delighted to get Henry Ford as a bag. Like every good caddie, I prided myself on my ability to make "a quick read of my bag," the key to a good tip. Caddying for Henry Ford added bounce to my step. I increased the enthusiasm of my "Yes, sir." On the second hole, a long par four reachable by only a very few players, Mr. Ford asked me, after hitting what was a very good drive for him, whether he could get home from where he lay. I replied, "Not in one." He delighted in my answer. He shared it with the other players in the group. I concluded that he wanted a comic, and a comic I would be. My chance came again on the fourth hole, a short par four, dogleg right. Having driven wickedly into the woods on the right and thus blocking any possible advance of his ball, Mr. Ford asked what he should do. I replied, repeating a golf joke I had read in *Reader's Digest*, "Pray!" Mr. Ford didn't find my remark at all funny. In fact, he was clearly insulted. He refused to talk to me during the rest of the round. My tip for the eighteen was the all-time caddie house low of fifty cents. When my grandmother later told me how my grandfather had been sprayed with firehoses by Ford's goons when he went for a job at Ford's before the First World War, I concluded the Fords and my family just weren't cut out for each other.

In the '54 National Amateur, the biggest golfing event of the club's history and my caddie life, I experienced disappointment. My bag was a stocky, pock-marked man in his late thirties or early forties, a restaurant owner from Los Angeles whose name I have forgotten. He had none of the promise of the exciting, wild-hitting, brilliantly recovering Billy Joe Patton, the well-known Charlie Coe, the emerging Arnold Palmer, or the sleek, flashy, silver-haired English aristocrat, Robert Sweeny—my friend Ron's bag. (Sweeny, finishing second to Palmer, had tuned up for the Amateur in the Winter of 1953 by playing down south with Claude Harmon and Ben Hogan.)

Yet my bag followed a first-day bye with a brilliant round the next day. He closed out his opponent on the fourteenth hole, well on his way toward a course record. I clubbed him perfectly and lined up his putts flawlessly. I shared his happiness. The next day, my advice was as bad as his play. On the par-four eleventh hole, I insisted he hit an eight rather than a nine iron, which he wanted to take. He hit the ball over the green and into the rough. By the sixteenth hole he was done for. I felt I had failed him. He gave me a two dollar tip for each round of play and practice, for a total of fourteen dollars in all. My friend, Ron, received five hundred dollars from runner-up Sweeny. I was jealous.

Work at the country club was, for me, an education in class. Uniformed blacks manned the locker room, foyer, bar and grill, and half-way house. Italians manned the pro shop, the clubroom, and the caddie shack, while predominantly working class and lower-middle class kids filled out the ranks of caddies. Names like Standish, Lord, Chesebrough, and Higbie headed the membership list, and I was unaware at the time just how English they were.

Work at the club also taught me about generosity. Pro Joe Belfore trusted me to run and manage the driving range my junior and senior years in high school. On the range, where I worked from one o'clock in the afternoon until sundown from Spring through Fall, I was allowed to hit all the balls I wanted. With each shot, I carried on my most important conversations with myself, asking, "Could I become a pro?" with the sincerity only a young boy could muster.

Friend & Enemy

As I progressed from being a freshman on the Denby High School golf team to the captain of its 1956 city championship team, I measured myself by this dream of being a professional golfer. Golf was my pride and love. I knew its rules far better than those of math, which I flunked, or biology, English, and Spanish, in which I received D's during my first two disastrous years in high school.

School days turned into semesters and semesters turned into years, nothing exciting ever seemed to happen for me. Whereas on the course, everything was exciting—and it was all about me: my aim, sight, judgment, swing, and score. In boring classes, I played imaginary rounds of golf. I played them at the country club, as redesigned by Robert Trent Jones in 1952 to bring the club up to the championship standards dictated by metal-shafted clubs, livelier balls, and the forthcoming National Amateur. The country club was a real test, even though it had relatively wide fairways and average-sized greens without large humps or subtle breaks. The course's difficulties (which appear even now when I play the course in my mind) were its large, deep, and abundant bunkers that, with great variation, surrounded almost all of its greens; its many strategically-placed fairway bunkers, whose sides and backs were covered with rough; and the stroke-costing rough and trees lining several fairways. Above all else, it had testing par fours that required accuracy off the tee and equal accuracy on two-hundred-yard-long second shots to trapped, elevated greens with narrow entrances, deep roughs, and traps in the back. From the professional tees, the second, seventh, twelfth, and fourteenth holes were 450 yards and, for the '54 Amateur, the par-five ninth and seventeenth holes were also converted into par fours.

Once I almost bent the country club course to my will. In the final round of our caddie tournament, I experienced the ecstasy of magic putting. I aimed and the ball went in. I made six or seven birdies in the thirty holes it took to me to win. I was master of my game that day. However, on most days, the course loomed over me like a great mountain that I could not scale. It imposed itself on me with the crushing thought that I could never consistently shoot par. Hence, I could never be a championship golfer.

A sense of my limits was reinforced by my poor play in the Detroit regional caddie tournaments. To this day, I remember how poorly I played on the world-famous Oakland Hills Country Club in Birmingham. I went to this course with trepidation. Its pro, Al Watrous (probably better remembered for his last hole British Open loss to Bobby Jones than for his wins) welcomed all, pros included, with the standing bet that they couldn't break 80 their first time out. If that wasn't enough to spark dread in me, I went to the course with an alibi: My arms were still sore from a fight the previous day.

With three really ugly shots, I reached the green of the par-four first. Then, on its immense and subtle green, I four-putted. Things didn't improve after that. With all its traps, its contoured holes and greens, and its long par fours and par fives, this course struck me as a replica, in many ways, of our Country Club of Detroit. However, its greater length, hills, rolling fairways, and quick, tiered greens, made it seem a more monstrous version of our course. Only later did I find out that it, too, had just recently been redesigned by Robert Trent Jones. Preparing it for the 1951 Open, Jones added his signature long, demanding par fours and par fives to a course originally designed by Donald Ross (Ross's home course was the great demonic northern Scottish course, Dornoch, and his own mentor was none other than Tom Morris of St. Andrews). I was brought to my knees without knowing anything of the impressive genealogy of this monster. I remember how leg and mind weary I was on its closing holes. I willingly accepted a double bogey on the eighteenth, glad just to end my misery. I posted a 97, a score which was ten shots higher than I had shot in the previous year.

So, golf's bondage caused me pleasures and pains. It could not have been otherwise, given my aspirations and the game's terrible allure. Most rounds disappointed my standards, but being young and in love with the game, I rebounded quickly from a bad round. My hopes were always easily reignited. I needed only a day or two of recuperative forgetfulness. And then, with a few swishes of my driver, as though it were a magic wand, I would again dream of being a professional.

I constantly sought perfection in my game. When I had free
time at home, I practiced my swing and chipped in the back-
yard. Between loops at the course, I went down to the old
hole and practiced. I never missed playing on caddie's day. We
started close to sunrise and had to play around the sprinklers
and putted many evenings until dark.

I was always among the first to open the golf season at
Chandler Park. One year I played between mounds of melt-
ing snow and on the frozen fairways. At school I even practiced gripping my pencils as if they were clubs and played
countless imaginary rounds as teachers droned on about tedious subjects. My obsession with the game increased during
that junior year in high school when I began to run the driving range. I don't know why I got the chance to run the range.
Perhaps it was because I was the best caddie-player. Perhaps
Joe Belfore (Belfiore, "beautiful flower," was his Italian name,
my Dad told me), who was head-pro at the club from 1934 to
1963, decided to help a fellow Italian.

On the driving range, I would practice hour after hour. I
learned to hit long, short, high, and low shots, along with
fades, hooks, and shots from different lies. There I observed
the assistant pros up close. I took their free advice. I even tried
to master (to no good effect) the complex, body-contorting
keys to Hogan's swing. I spent days trying to take the club
back slowly, keeping my right elbow in, aiming my club at the
target, pronouncing the set of my left knee (an idea from assistant pro, Ray Milan, that betrayed me by breaking the
rhythm of my downswing), and taking the club back straight
as a one-piece motion for the first foot before lifting it up.
The latter suggestion, which was a useful idea from Larry
Tomasino, considerably increased my distance, although, if
exaggerated, it led to the stiffening of the forearms and the
stopping of the body turn.

On the range there were days of ecstasy, when my swing found its tempo and rhythm. I could hit any shot out of nearly any lie. The best shots became routine. I became momentarily confident that I could not miss—I would be a pro.

Such highs were usually followed by disappointing lows. New expectations spawned new pains. Having on the range all the balls I wanted to hit, I was like a glutton with too much food before him. I would practice until the calluses on my hands split and started to bleed. The better I hit my shots, the better I expected to hit them. It was as if the closer I approached my goal, the further it receded from me. And worst of all were the times, which were frequent, when a good practice session was followed by terrible play. I would stumble off the course feeling betrayed, disgusted, and nauseated. I experienced a new range of disturbing emotions that I, a mere boy, had no language for, and I hurt in new ways.

At times, I felt as if I had two swings—one for the driving range and another for the course. A few times I quit playing for a week or ten days. I even reasoned that if laying off made me feel better, why not quit altogether? I suffered golf alone and was too proud to acknowledge that a game could get me so down. I never thought of taking the matter up with a priest, though, to play golf perfectly, I would have understood the temptation of Faust and his decision to sell his soul.

Golf, my sole pleasure, punished me uniquely. Believing I must "make it" by age eighteen or not at all, and running out of faith that practice would make the decisive difference, I experimented with changes of attitude. First, I tried willed optimism, fashionable because of the book by the Reverend Norman Vincent Peale, *The Power of Positive Thinking*. If, Peale taught, I expected good shots, I would get good shots. When this forced optimism failed, as it quickly did, I substituted the reverse attitude of a consistent, thorough-going pessimism: I would play expecting the bad in hopes of being surprised by the good. Almost instantaneously, I got the bad I expected and quickly abandoned the experiment of successful golf by attitude.

Golf humiliated me. I was bewildered by this game that I could not outplay or outthink, as I had neither the physical nor the mental resources necessary for success. Once, facing a relatively simple second shot on the fifteenth hole (where Billy Joe Patton of North Carolina had made a great four from the back of the green off some grass clippings to stay in the '54 Amateur), I dedicated a second shot to the shapely blonde who accompanied me on my round of golf. She made my blood pulse as few other girls had. I would express my love with a fine shot. I hit it fat. It flew feebly and landed smack in the center of the giant sand trap that guarded the front of the green. Although she was sweet to kiss, my shot augured our relationship accurately. However, no humiliation was as great as losing the caddie championship in my senior year. I lost it to a caddie a year my junior, whose last name was D'Amato. Smaller, younger, with a name derived from mine, and an odd swing to boot, he suggested that I was already being supplanted by the younger generation.

I began to think increasingly of golf as an enemy from whose illusions I had to free myself. The more I wanted happiness, the more miserable I became. With almost Buddha-like enlightenment, I came to recognize that the promise of golf's pleasures chained me to its pains. My growing pessimism was voiced in the first lines of poetry I ever wrote:

Some men strive
To discover life a meaningless hive.
While others crave
To find it a bottomless grave.

In retrospect, I can now see that I was trading golf's promise of glory for a new-found pride in thinking. If I could not defeat golf on the course, I would encompass it by understanding. While I continued to play—and at times even played well—I began to steadily distance myself from the game. As I felt my own future pressing in on me, I took measure of my place in the game by observing the lives of the assistant pros at our course. It was apparent to me that they didn't get the money, respect, and, above all else, the glory I wanted. I found their subservience unappealing. I surmised that they may well have lost the most important bet of all: that of their lives.

I grew more interested in school and became determined to go college. I improved from a D+ to an A student. Golf no longer seemed to be the be-all and end-all of my life. Although our high school team won the city championship that year and I finished eighth out of two or three hundred regional golfers (finishing the last eighteen with a 72), golf gave way to reading and a new-found high school popularity that made me the class officer of a senior class of approximately six hundred students. I found that in the world of knowledge (formed my senior year by the subjects of chemistry, literature, and history), my efforts were rewarded by steady and cumulative growth.

Golf's hold over me was broken when I was awarded a four-year scholarship for my tuition and room at the University of Michigan. It was the wonderful Standish-Evans caddie scholarship (started in the nation by the great golfer Chick Evans and implemented in our region by our own club's Mr. James Standish, Jr.) My father was really proud. I was doing what he would have done, if he had been given the chance. I was the first in my family to attend a university. I was ready to explore the pleasures of knowledge and to compete for happiness on another terrain. So I put my clubs in the closet and they were rarely taken out until my graduate study was completed ten years later. The university became my new garden of pleasure and pain.

Golf Becomes an Old Friend

At the University of Rochester in the spring of 1966, with my doctoral examinations in history completed, with no job prospects in sight, and filled with anxiety about my upcoming August wedding, I got out my old Guldahl woods (1, 3, and 4), and went out to a nearby municipal public course in the river park. There I bought a second-hand set of Tommy Armour irons for $60 dollars, and started playing low-stakes skins games with a small group of friendly black players. They welcomed me on the condition that I would bet something. I found that I was still not the worst public links player out there and was secretly delighted when they declined to give me strokes. I can't say I made any money, but a few pars and birdies stiffened my wavering resolve to get married, which has had the wonderful consequence of providing me with a loving mate for the past twenty-eight years.

During the first years of marriage, I again put my clubs away. Nearly the next time I got them out was in 1975, when I was on sabbatical in Riverside, California. I went to a nearby course and bought a new set of MacGregor irons and woods, though I never quite got the hang of, nor came to like, the narrow California canyon courses. Unplayable lies among rocks were the price of driving off the fairway. Nevertheless, golf had again served me well. It had distracted me from my books.

The following year, when I returned home to Minnesota, I embraced golf fully. Our small regional college was caught up in acrimony spawned by four years of topsy-turvy growth that was followed by four years of precipitous decline. Few feuds can be as nasty as university fights, which are fueled by free time, surplus vanity, high-blown presumptions, and individuals unrivaled in making mountains out of mole hills. I, who had helped form the university teachers' union, began to play golf to get away from continuing conflict at work. Crisp, strong prairie winds on the golf course cleansed my soul.

Golf offered me an escape into a miniature world. It offered no other significance than the play itself. In contrast to research and writing, golf yielded immediate pleasure. On the course, the only authorities are the rules of the game. I aimed, swung, saw, and scored. I enjoyed experiencing golf's connection between mind and body and took an epicurean-like pleasure in learning to hit different shots: shots that floated idly across space, those that bore their way into the wind, and those, as calculated, that bent, skidded, and rolled onto the green. I was enchanted by the wonderful shots that occasionally came off the face of my clubs. Their glorious flights—so straight, so high, so long, and accurate—surprised and delighted me. I was especially pleased by shots that I visualized perfectly before playing them, and then played them as I had seen them. They made me feel in contact with a higher order.

Such shots nearing perfection are remembered long afterward. For instance, I remember a shot worth a lifetime's memory. Playing directly into a strong wind on a long par-four, I hit the shot I envisioned. Out of a good lie, with the ball sitting up high, I drilled a 250-yard driver out of the rough. Dead on line, it landed just short of the green and rolled just past the cup. I missed the eight-footer coming back, but the keen fairway shot is a vivid, pleasurable memory. I also remember how twenty years ago on a course in Riverside, California, I hit a splendid sixty-yard trap shot,

which, cut thin, flew over sixty feet of sand, across another
thirty to forty feet of fairway, and across another ninety feet
of rising, rolling green. It landed and stuck only two feet from
the pin, saving my par. (That two greenskeepers witnessed the
shot added to my satisfaction.) I also remember my first hole-
in-one on the eighth hole of Detroit's municipal course, Red-
ford. A group waved us up on the short, uphill par three before they started to putt. I hit a five-iron shot that landed on
the front of the green, rolled straight for the cup at the back of
the green and went in. I remember a saving putt I made nearly
fifteen years ago on the par-three eighth at St. Andrews. I
sank a downhill, sidehill putt of fifteen feet that broke more
than twice that distance on the way to the cup. Had it not
sunk (though it couldn't have been rolling much slower), it
would have rolled off the green. I also remember "mistaken
epiphanies." On St. Andrews's very short tenth (called the
Bobby Jones Hole) I hit what I believed was a perfect drive
with a 4-wood, only to discover that it had come to rest in a
"wee bunker"—indeed, the tiniest pot bunker in all golfdom.

Far more than when I was young, I found myself playing
alone and enjoying it. I increasingly considered it not only a
special pleasure but a kind of honor to have a course to myself. I liked off-hours play, especially early evenings. I welcomed the Fall, when the temperature dropped into the 50s
and the wind swept all but die-hard players off the course.

I confess that I delight in being a solitary golfer. An empty
course (without other players and especially without carts) is,
for me, like a book to be written. I discover that the more I
golf, the more I write, and the more I write, the more I golf.
The course is a laboratory where I walk, play, and think.
Worlds of time exist between each shot.

My friend Don Olsen—a 1950s-era captain of the University of Minnesota golf team, who in his sixties can still play an

occasional fine round—wrote me of the matter of being a solitary golfer:

Solitary golf. Yes, this is the best golf of all. Out there alone you can be anything, you can play anywhere, you can do anything and everything. When I play alone, I move into a dream world that is my own, where truly magical and impossible shots occur. Even as lousy as I now play, I can hit the most astonishing shots when I am out there alone and move into another time warp, another galaxy of the self. I dare not describe them to you, else you would say I have finally stepped off the edge and gone mad and am beyond repair and have become the world's greatest liar.

If I have time, I frequently drive thirty miles north of home to the small nine-hole course at Canby. Though stranded on the Minnesota prairie, it has the feel of a Scottish seaside links course. Its layout is eccentric; its condition is primitive. Strong winds constantly play across its gently rolling and undulating terrain, which is seasonally colored by subtle changes of greens, browns, and golds, and is surrounded by tall grass fields. There are rarely more than a few players on the course, at least on most weekday mornings, and I am allowed to be alone with my game. There, I am in touch with the pleasures of golf from an earlier time.

My usual escape is to my home course in Marshall, where the pro has nicknamed me "Back Nine Joe" as a commentary on my solitary play. A decent eighteen-hole test, especially after recent improvements, it has adequate length and steady winds, a number of fairway bunkers, a meandering river, some well-placed ponds, and several large, interesting greens.

I need only arrive on its first tee and I am happy. As I walk, I feel the wonderful sense of my body in tireless motion. I love the feel of clubs riding on my shoulders. Even on the highly-manicured, chemically-treated grounds of the course, there is nature. On the eleventh and eighteenth holes, which are parallel to each other, Purple Martins, riding the winds with tilting bodies and tipping wings, make me part of their game, circling me, seeing which can come closest. Now and then a hawk circles above, and once in a while I am surprised by a great heron rising up from the muddy shoals of the river.

Frequently, my solitary rounds turn into practice sessions. Sometimes I hit as many as three balls after a single miss. On occasion, I end up playing a two-ball tournament against myself. With each good shot, there comes the immediate pleasure of feeling myself strike a ball as it should be struck, and the satisfaction of knowing few could strike the shot any better. I fly with the ball I strike.

Occasionally I compete. A skins game is always pleasurable. It allows the stimulating pressure of trying to tie a hole and the frequent chance to go for it with no regard for the consequences of a failed shot. Competition with someone else—or simply the presence of another—adds a note of excitement to my play. I particularly enjoy the rivalry with my friend John Meyer, a former college golfer, which has swung back and forth with near pendulum-like regularity between matches and across whole seasons for over fifteen years. I also enjoy rivalry with my son, Adam, a former high school and college golfer. We have played together at home and twice overseas. There was a special joy involved in our two trips to Britain and Ireland, playing such equally great courses as the Royal North Devon, Porthcawl, Ballybunion, the Royal Liverpool, the Royal Birkdale, and Prestwick. A round of golf is a sacrament we share.

Like a bird of migration, I accept the call every two or three years to go to the British Isles to play. I treat these migrations as pilgrimages. There I search out the secrets of the game and the joys of my own youth. Like old lovers getting together in a romantic place for a weekend, I find the wind, rough, seascape, the primitive quality of the links—and yes, the absence of carts—reinvigorating. I return home with rekindled desire and play heartily again. I have a particular fondness for Prestwick, which I have played the most and take to be the Devil's home course.

Golf is my singing, painting, woodworking, and gardening. Having learned to play as a boy, clubs are tools my hands know well. By virtue of years of play, I know the game's techniques and lore. The game is my body; I feel it in my hands. The game connects me back to my youth, when my pleasures were freshest and were written most indelibly on my senses. As a man, I yield to the boy within me.

As a boy and now a man, I find that I cannot easily separate my awareness of myself from golf. It shapes my feelings about such basic things as the wind, the grass, the landscape, and my body itself. Golf informs my senses of distance, aiming, and power. Golf for me is about flight, landing, touch, softness, roll, finesse, waiting, and precision. It influences my notions of excitement, risk, pressure, and competition. And it instructs me in patience, control, and even grace. Through golf I experience the world.

To anticipate Spring's approach, I begin to swing a club indoors and practice putting. It is as if my magic strokes will elevate the sun, warm the earth, melt the winter's snows, turn grasses green, and open the links. If I yielded to the temptation of ordering my view of heaven to serve my earthly pleasures, upon checking in there, I would ask for clubs and balls, instructions to the nearest course, and a slight breeze.

1

A Horizon of Pleasures

ALTHOUGH GOLF HAS MANY PLEASURES, surely the first
pleasures experienced are about feel. Golf is about the grip,
the heft and swish of a club; about striking a ball and the first
sight of its lofted flight. Its most elemental pleasures are feels
associated with its required strokes, which range from the
subtlest chips and pitches to delicate half-cuts and knocked-
down hooks, from great blasts out of roughs and traps to high
booming tee shots with fade for gentle landings or spinning
hooks for long runs. These strokes account for a rich spec-
trum of bodily pleasures involving hands, ears, and eyes. The
body experiences itself during the swing. There are keen bodily pleasures associated with the golf swing at every point: the
rhythm of the footwork; the turn of the body; the extension,
constriction, and unleashing of the muscles; the mounting
power of the swing; and the fullness of the follow-through
and its relaxation.

We can inventory these many bodily pleasures of golf by
describing an imaginary round. First of all, the player is up,
out, and about. Henry Leach wrote in *The Happy Golfer,*

Here on the links are space and freedom such as are afforded to people, especially those of towns and cities, rarely in the present time. Confinement is a wearing oppression to the modern man. Through the medium of this sport, we may experience the sense of space and freedom, of something that comes near to infinity. Unconscious of this cause, a golfer on the links is uplifted to a simpler freer self.

On the course, the golfer is variously stimulated, aroused, alert, and excited. A player's cleats click rhythmically on the pavement and gravel path. This rhythm is joined to the jangling of clubs responding to the player's gait. He moves out onto the soft, manicured grass of the tee and nervously sizes up the first hole. There is the bright sound of the bag being unzipped and a fumbling search for balls, which always feel surprisingly hard, and the brightly-colored, garishly mismatched tees. The glove feels tight to his hand and gives a sense of security. These preparatory acts are pleasurable and bring expectations of further pleasure once the round begins.

Waiting

Golf involves all different kinds of waiting. Waiting enhances the stimulation that pleasure requires. The player waits for the clearing of the first tee, then for the opening of the first fairway. The player begins his swing by making a few nervous anticipatory waggles as he seeks to set his concentration and establish the flow of his backswing. The swing actually forms itself out of these preliminary motions that anticipate it. There is the wait for the club to reach the top of its arc. At the top of the swing, there is a precious moment's hesitation before starting down. Then there is the instant before impact, and then the player waits for the shot to rise up before him and take flight toward its target.

Waiting is necessary for pleasure. Yet at some point, intense waiting turns to pain and even agony. Nothing is as long as the wait for the putt that circles the cup to drop. Little eternities cluster in such waits. The player must often wait as he works his way around the course. He waits for the posting of scores and suffers out the long night before the tournament's start. This agony defeats more than one player before he arrives on the first tee. And, for the contender, waiting stretches across seasons.

In *Second Shots*, Bernard Darwin described how often the golfer cannot abide waiting.

> *Very often, more especially when we are nearing the end of a match, we neglect the way of safety, not because we do not realise its value, but because we have not the strength of mind to prolong the agony. If we play safe there is still another trial in front of us in the shape of the final little pitch, and we are not brave enough to wait for it. We want to be out of our misery, and so, out of pure cowardice, we take the unjustifiable risk. If all goes well we try afterwards to pretend that we had another motive, that over-cautious tactics might have been defeated by a long steal of the enemy. We may even brazen it out successfully to a criticising friend, but we cannot deceive ourselves.*

Feelings & Sensations

On the first tee, the player, alert with expectation, hopes for and dreads the first shot of the round. He grips his club and begins lightly swinging it back and forth, setting his hands, arms, shoulders, torso, legs, and feet in motion, a way of gently reminding his body what it knows of the game. The player sinks his tee into the soft ground and places his ball upon it. He steps back and takes a few more practice swings, all the while surveying the hole, imagining the shot he wants to hit. Then he sets up, digs in, waggles again, and the swish of the swing is followed by the crack of his shot, and the sight of the rising ball.

Many of the pleasures a golf round occasions are intimate to the feel and the movement of the player's body. There are the subtle instinctual pleasures of adjusting the body to its correct position at address, as if one is snuggling up with oneself. Making the varied strokes (hard and soft, full, three-quarters, and half) required by different shots makes use of the hands, wrists, arms, shoulders, hips, legs, and feet in instinctive and automatic coordination with one another.

When the golfer strikes the ball, he experiences golf's greatest pleasure. Squeezed within a fraction of a second, the player feels the ball on the club face. Within that instant, there is a variety of distinct pleasures associated with force, power, gracefulness, completion, and relief. There are a variety of ways of striking the ball. They range—to suggest only a few—from the feel of crunching a drive, to swinging full and through a long-drawn or a high-faded fairway wood, to ripping a low long iron and striking down with a midiron, to a gently flopped sand shot and a delicately touched downhill chip. Each type of shot produces a distinct sensation, with its own sight, sound, and feel.

The vividness of striking a ball explains why some golfers prefer to spend their time on the practice range, where there are no delays between shots. The distinct pleasure of hitting a single type of shot explains why many players tend to practice the shot they hit best. Older players are actually soothed by hitting a type of chip shot over and over again. (After an arguement with Aunt Milly, my Uncle Dale would go out in his back yard and practice chipping sand wedge shots in their daughter's sandbox until his anger subsided. We used to say

we could tell how well Dale and Milly were getting on by observing how much sand remained in Cindy's sandbox.)

As the player's head comes up, completing his swing, he has
the additional pleasure of seeing the shot just struck. A golf
ball can move through space in a multitude of ways. It flies,
lines, kites, soars, and bores; it bounces, hops, skips, rolls; it
spins, sticks, bites, and backs up; it curves, swerves, wobbles,
turns, swirls, and falls. Each of these motions captivates the
human eye and awakens distinct feelings associated with the
terror, sublimity, beauty, dignity, humor, and even farce that
humans experience upon observing the movement of things.

The first par-five hole of our imaginary round alone produces an array of sensations of eye, ear, body, and touch. On
the second shot, there is the slashing sound of the long iron
swing, which tears the ball out of the rough, and the accompanying sight of a ball hit on a line-drive trajectory. The third
shot, a hundred-and-fifty-yard eight iron from the center of
the fairway, produces the deep thud of the descending blow of
the short iron swing as it digs into the turf and quickly elevates the ball. Carrying backspin, the ball hits the green.
Then, seeming to momentarily defy the laws of motion, it
stops, before beginning gently to accelerate backwards.

On the next hole of our imaginary round, the player seeks
to pick a ball out of a fairway trap without touching the sand.
For an infinitesimal instant, the player feels as if he succeeded.
The ball has been firmly struck. No sand has been taken. Yet,
almost instantaneously, there is the sickening sound (a sound
every player knows) of the ball nicking the lip of the trap as it
exits. With his head up, he sees the ball slicing short and right
of the green into a deep bunker that protects the front right
corner of the green. He imagines, as if he could feel across a
great distance, that his ball has sunk deeply into the sand and
upon arriving at the trap discovers his instincts were correct.
Seeking to recover, the player drives his wedge as deeply and

as hard as he can into thick, wet sand in order to explode his ball over the high lip of the trap and onto the green. From the grass apron collaring the green, where his ball ended up, he hits a delicate pitch shot. At first, it appears as if he will be short, but somehow his ball keeps rolling. His whole body reacts to his ball as it slides past the cup, picks up momentum, and finally stops, leaving him with a difficult nine-foot sidehill putt for par. He calculates the green. It is hard and quick. He examines the tilt of the cup. He looks for irregularities and spike marks around the cup. On course, spinning well (as if it is driven by the sharpness and clarity of his intention), his putt moves back up the hill and toward the hole. It's as if his ball has eyes. It appears, to his exultation, to enter the cup only to somehow pop back up and out. It rode the rim of the cup, exiting it at the very point at which it entered and an eternity was felt to transpire while the shot rode the lip. The shot ended in disappointment, yet it provided a rush of sensations, feelings, and emotions, which took the player's soul out of its ordinary state.

Among golf's first bodily pleasures is the sense of graceful motion. The good swing itself delights the golfer, as the good step pleases the dancer, or the successful jump or spin delights the skater. The grip on the club, when neither too firm nor too weak, produces a sense of ordered harmony in the hands themselves. The turn of the legs and coil of the back impart a sense of power. The movement of the golfer's feet and legs, the gentle glide of his hips towards the target, and finally the breaking of his wrists, when in proper sequence and uninterrupted by abrupt interventions of consciousness, produce a sense of a flow, accelerating speed, and mounting power. The follow-through culminates the swing and joins the pleasing sensations of lightness, control, speed, power, and flow.

The swing's forms vary from the long, full drive to the short pendulum, stiff-wristed chip and putt. Combining

rhythm, tempo, and flow, the good swing is a graceful movement that for a most pleasing moment, like the swish of a
magic wand, takes the golfer outside himself and delivers him
into a realm of grace, where body and mind touch.

Every golfer, even those who slash and hack at the ball, is in
love with his own swing. Every club has a swing narcissist,
who, on and off the course, constantly practices his swing. I
remember "Never-Play Joe" at Chandler Park, who hung
around the clubhouse and putting green all day practicing his
swing. He usually didn't even have a club in his hands and
rarely ever hit a ball, yet he was constantly swinging.

The Pleasing Garden

As the player progresses around the course, all his pleasures
are not of swing and shot alone. The course itself is a pleasant
garden. The course emerges from and submerges into the
landscape. The hilly, bubbly greens and sandy-brown fairways and roughs of the seaside links course especially fill the
golfer's eye. Robert Hunter describes the particular variations
and pleasures of the seaside links courses and their subtle undulations:

> At Prince's and St. Georges one plays in and out of great
> swales lying between huge dunes, and now and then one is
> forced to cross the dunes. But at Deal, St. Andrews,
> Hoylake, and Westward Ho! one has the feeling of playing
> over comparatively flat land. There is little climbing and
> yet in the play one rarely finds the ball on an exact level
> with the feet. . . . To play golf there requires a great variety
> of strokes, and the placing of one's second shot amidst such
> undulations in a manner to make them serve one is a source
> of never-ending delight. On the links the player has not
> only to deal with formidable hazards, but also with

countless little ones—those beautifully turfed, harmless looking undulations which run through the fairways from tee to green. Terrain of that sort will yield superlative golf anywhere.

Club selection on an undulating terrain is challenging. There, roll can be as important as flight. It is anything but mechanical: The player can't just read a yardage marker (a bush, a bunker, a colored round pad) and shoot away. He must consider how the green is best approached, and whether to miss right or left, short or long. On undulating terrain, he must consider all this in terms of what shot his lie naturally invites, might permit, or absolutely prohibits. For instance, the uphill lie, with the ball lower than the feet, will make a low draw hook almost impossible, even though the green invites that precise shot. Indeed, the lie may force the player to try a great shot because there is no other shot to be played, or, on the contrary, forbid the bold shot he believed his tee shot earned him or that his match requires. On the undulating terrain of the links the player gets pleasure from seeing his desire and reason war over what he wants to do and what can be done. Golf is a continuous test of calculation and judgment. The golfer must, on any given shot, measure and evaluate lie, wind, pin placement, alternative shots, cost of error, likelihood of a good shot, score to present, and winning score needed on the hole and for the round. On the links few compliments equal that of "Clever shot!" or "Well done!"

On his round the knowledgeable golfer has the additional pleasure of perceiving the architect's design of the course. He sees the variety of alternatives the course offers and the excitement, thrills, and suspense which go with that variety. Each well-placed hazard enhances a player's pleasure, as does the overall variation in the length and shape of its holes. In the words of golf course designer Alister MacKenzie (who designed the Masters course at Augusta National, Cypress Point, and the Royal Melbourne), "Variety is everything, or nearly everything."

When the Wind Is Up

Even the dullest course is improved immensely by the wind, even though it is commonly considered the golfer's worst enemy. When the wind is up, as it usually is on seaside links and prairie flatland courses, golf is at its best. In the wind everything is made more difficult. Holes normally requiring short irons to get home demand long irons, woods, or simply cannot be reached at all. While lies might invite the player to work the ball one way, the winds frequently insist he play it another way. Downwind shots, even the shortest, become the most testing to keep on the green. With wind all around the player's ears and a need to multiply the break because of the wind, the shortest putts become uncommonly difficult. A links player finds himself at war during the entire round—and this war counts as one of the game's greatest pleasures.

As much as the player can sense himself at battle against a course, he can also be surprised by its beauty and tranquility. Even on the wildest course on a windy day, he can experience a great calm. This is most likely to occur at twilight when the landscape is free of sharp contrasts and one senses, with the coming darkness, a quieting equality.

From an elevated tee the player spies out below him irregularly spaced small bands of fellow players working themselves across a shadowed and patched landscape of browns and greens. On the tee's promontory, the player feels that he belongs to a gentle community, whose sole and benign end is the many pleasures of a peaceful game.

These meditative moments, of course, soon give way to the more immediate pleasures of aiming, swinging, and hitting.

He cautions himself that a slow swing is better in the wind. He drills the ball into the wind with a low hook to gain the extra yards of roll he needs on the long par five he faces. On his second shot, he swings slowly, seeking a big long arc, intending to hit slightly up on the ball, so he will hit a high fade that will ride the wind and run to the wide open side of fairway from which the hole's large terraced green opens. With his next shot, he catches just enough turf on the tight, thin, sand-based fairway to put just a little breaking backspin on his long running chip. It slides gently down the embankment and begins a suspenseful movement along the crest of the large green. With his pants blowing in the wind, the breeze humming up under the brim of his hat and around the back of his head, his stroke stays steady and even. His ten-foot putt spins perfectly, without a wobble, faltering only momentarily before it produces the friendly swirl and joyous clunk of the sunk putt. Feeling large-chested, he strides off the green. He alone of the foursome got a birdie on this hole—and he knows few today will play the hole any better than he did.

A shot can please a player for a variety of reasons: it simply felt good, had a favorable outcome, allowed him to win, got him praise from someone he respects, or proved his practice was not in vain. A shot can please him because it was properly executed, was part of a sequence of good shots, or because it reminded him of the pleasures of a past round he had or of a hole he once played, or because it brings to mind the good he anticipates in future rounds because he believes he can hit that shot again. The pleasures of a golf shot may baffle the philosopher who might wish to build a view of all life on simple and identifiable orders of pleasure and pain. Indeed, the pleasures of a single shot can be too many to enumerate and too subtle to elucidate.

*"Golf is something of a passion, and passions
are of the blood and have nothing to do
with conveniences and rules of life."*
—Henry Leach, **The Happy Golfer**

2

Bettors, Buddhas, & Perfectionists

ALTHOUGH EVERY GOLFER is locked in a game against
himself, golfers have been traditionally divided into the two
distinct families of those whose pleasure is match play and
those who prefer medal play. The former, according to a con-
ventional distinction, have their delight in beating their opponent, while the latter prefer to defeat the course. In truth,
however, some of the best match players of the past (when
head-to-head play was of greater importance than medal play)
chose to ignore their opponent's game. They believed this
saved them from focusing their attention on the changing fortunes of their opponent, which could steal their concentration. A lot of fine match players contend the contrary, that to
not observe an opponent's shot, and play accordingly, is a sure
way to lose a match.

John Ball was a classic match player of yesteryear. Ball's
play made it clear why few responded to his father's challenge, "Me and my son will play any two!" Born in 1861 at

Hoylake, near Liverpool, Ball, when only fifteen, finished sixth in a British Open. Ball went on to win one British Open and eight British Amateurs, the seventh at Prestwick on the thirty-seventh hole and the eighth at Westward Ho! on the thirty-eighth. At Westward Ho! Ball was continually jeered as the representative of the upper classes by crowds committed to the victory of his working-class opponent, Abe Mitchell.

The outstanding American amateur, Robert Hunter, caught up with Ball at Hoylake for a match in 1912 just after Ball's Westward Ho! victory. In the two rounds they played together, Ball continually asked Hunter for halves, or a tie on the hole, when his shots lay twice as far from the cup as Hunter's. In one case, Ball even asked for a half when Hunter was on the green and he, Ball, was in a sand trap next to the green. Hunter denied Ball's requests, but won no holes by his denials. On the sixteenth, a par three, Ball lay twenty yards from the cup and Hunter a mere eight feet. Nevertheless, Ball asked for the fifth and last time for a half.

> *"Will you give me a half?"*
>
> *"But you can't ask for half here," I answered, "I have a putt for a two."*
>
> *"Well, I also have a putt for a two. And, remember, you promised me a half whenever I asked it. Will you give it?"*
>
> *"But this is absurd, and I refuse it."*
>
> *"Then you are not a man of your word."*
>
> *"No, I am not a man of my word."*
>
> *"You'll be sorry."*
>
> *And he proceeded to hole the long winding putt. After that I could not, of course, hole mine, and for the fifth time in thirty-six holes Johnny had done what seemed quite impossible. He was delighted, and left the club that evening in a glorious good humor.*

If there are special characteristics that make a good match player or not, the match player's primary pleasures are in the shots that let him win. Some match players are notorious gamesmen who try to unsettle, disturb, and confuse their opponents. For instance, they show up for the match just in the nick of time. They try to confuse their opponent about the club they used or how hard they hit their shot. They seek to induce fear in their opponent or unsettle him. They play "their man," not the course. In the old days when stymies were allowed (where the ball blocks the opponent's path to the cup and which were permitted in the game's official rules until approximately 1950), they would take as much pleasure in putting a good stymie on their opponent as any other shot they would hit in the match. Yet there is in the family of match players a different type of player, one who enjoys the match for the sake of the match. In fact, he takes so much pleasure in the rivalry of a good match that, even at the risk of losing it, he grants his opponent extra time to look for a lost ball, refuses to call a technical foul on his opponent, and even cheers for his opponent's good shots.

The preferred form of contemporary play, however, is medal play. It belongs to this more polite and sensitive present time when nicknames and gamesmanship are on the wane. Nevertheless, at points the pleasures of medal play are identical to match play. On his way to a tournament victory, the medal player may find himself battling head-to-head with only one or two other rivals. Playoffs invariably reduce themselves to a form of match play.

Players often remember tournaments not in terms of scores, but in terms of losing to or beating an opponent. Rivalries like that of Sarazen versus Hogan, or Hogan versus Snead, Nicklaus versus Palmer, or Watson versus Nicklaus, characterize decades of the game's best play.

If some players need a rival to play well, others need to bet in order to enjoy golf. Betting alone brings the game to life for them. Every shot, hole, or round becomes an occasion to bet. For serious bettors, the pleasure of each shot—one's own or one's opponent's—depends on its relation to a bet. A fine shot may be disregarded, since it doesn't influence the outcome of the bet; conversely, a bad shot can be the source of a great deal of delight if it assures a handsome payoff.

Golf bets reach bizarre and outrageous proportions. According to *Golfer's Miscellany,* John Ball, the Hoylake golfer just mentioned, wagered in 1907 that he could play his course in a dense fog in under 90, in two and one-quarter hours, and not lose a ball, all of which he accomplished. The greatest cross-country match in America (again according to *Golfer's Miscellany*) occurred in 1929 in South Carolina. Two brothers played a match that covered 36 miles, took 13 hours, resulted in the loss of 22 balls, and the use of eight caddies and official cars. One brother shot 780, the other 825.

Other mad bets have led to games played through cities and across all sorts of different terrains. They have involved the use of a single club, a baseball bat, a club or a pool stick. Some have required drinking on every hole. They have pitted golfers against archers, javelin throwers, and even fishermen. Additionally, freak matches have required players to wear suits of heavy armor, dropping balls out of airplanes and helicopters, and playing in the middle of the night or blindfolded.

Driven by sterner gods, the greatest pleasure for some golfers lies in perfecting their game. This can be a fatal disease in young players, who presume perfection to be an actual possibility. The disease, which can involve prolonged cases of sulking and pouting, manifests itself in youth with swearing, throwing clubs, and walking off the course in reaction to any bad, or even less-than-desired, shot. The young Bobby Jones was a club thrower. He threw clubs, in the words of Herbert

Warren Wind, "at helpless elm trees." Young Gene Sarazen also had a bad temper. After a round of bad putting, Sarazen, the assistant professional, put the putter (which he had borrowed from a member), in a vice and sawed it to pieces. Sarazen was fortunate to not have lost his job. Surely, golf provides ample material for a book featuring horrible displays of golf temper, with chapters such as "tournaments quit," "clubs thrown," and "awful vows and curses made."

Golfers have thrown clubs into trees, broken them over their knees, thrown them in lakes and ravines, and literally tried to punish and humiliate clubs by dragging them behind their cars or, taking my Uncle Dale's less destructive approach, of putting them in a cellar and not letting them out for weeks at a time. Don Olsen wrote me:

> *My friend was caddying for professional Marty Furgol in a pro-amateur. This was back in 1948 or 1949. On the third hole, Furgol faded an iron shot into a greenside bunker and in anger, Furgol flung his club out into the rough. "Go get the club, caddie," Furgol said. My friend, the caddie, replied to Furgol, "Go get it yourself. You threw the fucking thing." (My friend was a tough-looking, ex-Golden Glove boxer. Furgol did as he was told.)*

Perfectionists and false perfectionists, those bad players who pretend that they should have hit well shots they really could never hit well, account for many of the longest club throwers. They forever focus on how lacking their game is. A single mis-hit shot can send true perfectionists scurrying off to the practice range for hours. Like the religious brother or sister devoted to perfecting their souls, these golf aspirants magnify the smallest flaws into damning sins.

In contrast to those who lose their tempers are players intent on maintaining their composure no matter what occurs.

These unflappable Buddhas strive to be indifferent to the pains and pleasures of their transitory fortunes on the links. They make it a point to restrain their emotions. Players like Ben Hogan and his contemporary Byron Nelson both found perfection in the mechanical repetition of a swing and were known as the game's ice men. "Hogan," Mark McCormack wrote about his 1953 British Open win, "was the nearest thing Britain had seen to the perfect golfing machine."

Before the First World War, Walter Travis was "the ice man" of American golf. Travis started the game at the age of thirty-five. He approached it as a science to be learned and a craft to be mastered. Eight years later, in 1904, he was the first American ever to win the British Amateur. Jerry Travis, a boy of seventeen who was to meet Walter in head-to-head play in an invitational tournament in the same year, described "the old man" of American golf as a "master mechanic [who functioned] with the precision of a Swiss watch." Jerry attributed his third hole playoff win over Walter—a victory dubbed "the kid over the old man"—to practice, luck, and a loaned Schenectady putter (identical to the type of loaned putter the elder Travis had credited with his British Amateur victory). Jerry believed his victory was due to old Walter's rare let-down near the end of the match, presuming victory was already his.

Once pressure appears, the player's pleasures are altered. Nerves transform all human experience. Even the greatest players, who have adjusted to the rigors of tournament play, play with tension. Herbert Warren Wind wrote:

The men who are used to playing under fire have long ago harnessed their nervousness. They seldom lose because of a jumpy feeling in their stomach, and contradictory as it seems at first, they worry about not being worried, about becoming phlegmatic and missing that little tingle that keeps a player sharp and dangerous.

However, Wind added, let winning professionals move from a regular tournament to a major championship, such as the U.S. or British Opens, and they begin to sweat. Under pressure, space and time seem to be constricted; the mind is not open; muscles are tense. Players can experience a nauseating thumping inside themselves. They lose their lucidity and certainty. Their pleasures are squeezed down to the mere relief which comes with hitting a passable shot, of simply not letting a drive leak into the rough on the eighteenth hole.

A round's pleasures succeed and replace, or join and fuse to one another as the player moves from hole to hole. The satisfaction from any given shot derives in part from memory and expectations. Individual shots in a round become part of sequences of shots that determine the player's satisfaction or dissatisfaction with his developing game. By the end of the round, most of the pleasures derived from distinct shots, sequences of shots, and moods associated with them have been forgotten—or, at least, have been put out of the player's active mind. They have been subsumed by his overall play. Only the most stunning and bizarre shots linger on the mind.

The Delights of the Clubhouse

In the clubhouse another order of golfing pleasure begins. There golfers define, clarify, and readjust their round by rationalizations, exaggerations, and sometimes even outright lies. Here playing counts less and talking more. At our club we tell of the member who got, on the same day, a hole-in-one on the par-three fourth, two times in a row. A young girl at a nearby course got a hole-in-one the second time she ever played when her badly sliced tee shot bounced off a mower at the edge of the green and rolled into the hole.

Gene Sarazen reported how one day he and another member of his foursome made successive holes-in-one on the same hole. At the Prestwick clubhouse, no doubt, they tell how, on the first hole, a short par four, two players in a match hit five consecutive shots out of bounds. And on the same hole, a tee shot once went into a passing train and came back out onto the course. Or, again on Prestwick's first, a favorable bounce off the railroad tracks got a hung-over player a hole-in-one.

The clubhouse is also the place to tell tales of errant shots ending up in such bizarre places as pockets, bottles, shoes (which happened to Bobby Jones once), or anywhere else a ball can fit. And these stories are matched by tales of great recovery shots played out of trees, off roofs, or out of water. Sarazen once won a hole from a shot out of a half-way house. Having removed a refrigerator, he hit his second shot out the window and onto the green. In one recorded case, a player's errant drive landed in a stream and his ball was carried downstream three hundred yards before coming to rest on a sandbar from which he pitched his second shot onto the green of a par five for an easy birdie.

Once in the clubhouse, the great majority of players forget most of the shots and details of their round. They find their pleasure in having a drink, counting the money they won, and bragging, if ever so discreetly, about the good shots they hit. Some players even solicit pity for their bad shots. Clubhouses are filled with those who implore others to believe how much better they could have played if only they had putted well, missed a few more hazards, had not been disturbed by a greenskeeper, had not gotten two bad bounces, and had not suffered yet other great misfortunes.

One could not expect golfers, human as they are, to clearly delineate the realities of their experiences as that would detract from the pleasure they derive in describing their rounds of golf. After all, golfers play golf for enjoyment.

"A perfect shot fills the eye and is a thing of beauty."
—*Jerome Travis,* **The Fifth Estate**

3

Delights & Ecstasies

THE GOLFER SEEKS varied pleasures in his garden. It is
there that he takes aim at distant targets and hurls balls across
great spaces. He intends to play a succession of shots as if no
flaw of mind, or swing, or difficulty of lie, hazard, or course,
or ill-fortune could intervene. The golfer seeks what is not
common to this earth, a realm where there is a near unmedi-
ated connection between intention, action, and result.

Like the seeker of religious experience, the golfer pursues
an ecstatic state, the blessed condition of being out of, free
from, and beyond the ordinary world. (*Extasis* in Latin means
terror. Its Greek roots, *ek* and *histanai*, literally connote being
out of place; in Greek itself *existanai* means to drive one out
of his senses.) The golfer seeks pleasures beyond those of distraction, stimulation, sociability, and satisfaction. From golf,
he seeks more than the pleasures of competition and victory
that are associated with all contests of speed, endurance, and
strength. Rather, he seeks the ethereal pleasure of lofting a ball
up into the sky and commanding its flight across space to its

target. Free of hesitation and awkwardness, the golfer seeks to serve the vision of his inner eye.

Aiming

Luck brings the pleasure of fortunate shots to all golfers. Even the first round of a beginner can produce several lucky shots, even rare holes-in-one. A primitive delight comes from a shot ending up where it was intended to go, even if it gets there by an odd route, the result of a faulty blow, or by pure chance. A topped fairway iron running all the way to the green or a skulled iron shot going into the cup are shots that amuse the player because they defy fate; the results of these shots are sometimes better than the golfer's best-struck shots. Advanced golfers delight in lucky shots as well, even when they reach such bizarre lengths as a hole-in-one being scored by a ricochet off an animal, house, or rock; in one incredible instance, a hole-in-one was scored when an out-of-bounds shot landed on a moving truck, whose driver stopped the truck near the green, found the ball, and deposited it in the hole.

Like novices in other sports, beginning golfers play for luck. They find pleasure in winning. With winning comes the momentary exultation that they are better than somebody else and that the gods are smiling on them. Also, curious things happen on the course. For example, one player's dentures fell out when he was examining his lie on a slope above a bunker. The dentures hit his ball, dislodged it, and sent it rolling into a sand trap. His false teeth cost him a two-stroke penalty.

However, for accomplished golfers, the greatest pleasures come with proper execution of the intended shot. Correctly executing the intended shot satisfies a rudimentary sense of power. Similarly, it is experienced by the person who success-fully aims and throws a ball of paper into a distant wastebas-ket. Humans, be it David with his sling, Odysseus with his bow, or any pub dart player, take great pleasure in projecting an object accurately through space. A strike or bull's eye makes them, in a way, lords of the earth for a moment.

As the success of all players of games that have targets or goals testifies, humans take great delight in aiming. There is an elemental pleasure in taking sight at something and hurling an object towards it, such as throwing a stone at a flying bird, hitting a rabbit on the run with a sling shot, or pitching a ringer in horseshoes.

There is almost endless fulfillment in aiming and shooting. Players of games will repeat the act of aiming and shooting over and over again, even when the likelihood of success is as-tronomically small. Proving that the human mind is not, as some have argued, the enemy of repetition, humans will wile away hours trying to throw balls through hoops, kick balls into nets, shoot arrows or bullets at targets, bat stones across distant fences, or flip and stick knives into trees.

The fascination of aiming includes a range of human activi-ties. Going to the depths of our animal nature, it is an activity we share with the hunting dragonfly, the spitting lizard, the striking snake, the attacking shark, or the diving hawk. As el-emental as it is for all living things to have targets, aiming is also for us humans associated with acts of reasoning and judg-ment. For the golfer, there is particular fulfillment involved in calculating and judging the best path to the target.

In some instances, the golfer's aim is immediate, or nearly so, as it occurs with the first sight of lie and target. It is as if lie and target together determine the shot's sole and just path. Reasoning, guessing, and judging are not required when a mere single glance joins the club, stance, and swing to the target. There is only one infallible path to the target and nothing interrupts the connection between target and mind. The shot is either made or isn't made.

On the contrary, a player's first perceptions can be unclear, confused, and even contradictory. The player adjusts his sight, recalculates his distance, rethinks his lie, feels forced to choose one of two or three different pathways to his target, and he still remains with no compelling reason to choose any one of them. The golfer pauses in his club selection, adjusts and readjusts his stance, recalculates the distance, and considers what might go wrong with any one shot. Yet, he still remains without a vision to swing to. Aiming in this case is simply guess and approximation.

Recently I chipped three balls at a fourth ball lying sixty to eighty feet away on the eighteenth green. The first was eight feet to the left; the second, one foot to the left; the third stopped next to and touched the ball. With each shot I had improved. Aiming in this case was a matter of calculation and adjustment. Yet, any golfer could cite countless times when his first shot, instantly seen and unhesitatingly hit, was superior to all his subsequent efforts. So aiming seems almost of two entirely different natures—one form of aiming is constructive, hypothetical, and experiential, the other is intuitive and unmeditated. Even the longest drive must have a target, even if the target is something as small as a patch of grass 265 yards from the tee on the left edge of the fairway, for without such a target both the player's concentration and aim will be flawed.

Indeed, the most cunning of golfers seek advantageous misses far more than perfect shots. They play golf knowing on which side of the fairway, the green, and the cup their shots, well or poorly hit, must end up. One of our club's best golfers always told his partner, "Miss right!"

Good golfers feel their superiority to nature because they move themselves and objects as projections of their own will. Because they can move objects according to their plans, they conjure and implement complex chains of actions and, in the process, take delight in knowing themselves to be makers of events. Golfers engaged outwardly in the humble business of hitting a ball around a course can actually experience a kind of earthly transcendence.

Uncommon Connections

The best golf shots are effortlessly hit, as if the golfer himself was an instrument of higher purpose. Body, swing, and club are felt to be as one, and the sensation is one of striking the ball without hitting it.

My friend Don Olsen wrote me of his experience on the sixteenth hole at the Little Falls Country Club.

The sixteenth is a par 3, about 185 yards, the green sitting well below the tee box. Two ponds guard front left and front right part of the green. The gadget of my [new found] swing gives me a slight fade. If I aim a 3-iron at the edge of the left-hand pond, the ball should fade just enough to land in the opening between the two ponds and bounce up towards the pin, hidden behind the right-hand pond.

The twosome in front waved me up. I took a lazy practice swing and it felt perfect. Suddenly, I became the shot. My entire sense of being became the shot. I, myself, was going to soar off towards the edge of that pond, slowly bend in towards the opening and land safely and bounce up towards the hole. Actually hitting the ball and seeing the result exactly as I had envisioned was almost redundant. Of course it was going to bounce up and stop six feet from the hole. The twosome waiting at the side of the green applauded and waved to me as the ball did exactly that. Surely, this was something of an out-of-body experience. Indeed, I had become the golf shot if only in my imagination and my memory. It was a journey, however brief, as real as any other.

The player knows himself to be the author of the shot, but he knows equally well it is not his shot. He experiences more the pleasure of being its agent rather than its owner. The player knows a good shot has been played. From earth to sky and back to earth, his shot formed a complete whole. His great pleasure is to have been a part of something that was perfect.

The Eye of Flight

It is easy to lend mystique to the golf shot, as it contains the mysterious elements of aim and flight which affect our spirit in primordial ways. No sooner does the eye (genetically shaped since the first animal eye to see, follow, and track) pick up a flying object, than the human mind itself soars to fly with it. With its instinctive sympathies, undeliberated or re-pressed, the mind bends inside itself with the long curving shot, and turns within itself to fly with the circling hawk. As flight awakens in us a passion to join it, so intended flight awakens an equally strong passion for accuracy. The human mind is quick to pick up the pattern of a flying object sketched out against the background of the sky. Once the eye catches sight of an object that is following an arc, the mind, as a matter of immediate instinct, cheers the flying object along the *correct* path to its target. An aesthetic requirement buried deeply inside us shapes our senses of just, proper, and beautiful motion. There are many pleasing paths of motion: they can be straight, curved, efficient, elegant, and even graceful, but they cannot be faltering and erratic if they are to please us. The mind instinctively urges the flying ball (even an opponent's shot) to its target, much as it cheers the plummeting hawk to fall and strike its hapless victim.

The novice has not sufficiently evolved as a golfer to fully appreciate the range of pleasures associated with the graceful shot. He cannot, either as player or observer, conceive the shot that is necessary for him to hit, imagine the swing that does the inner mind's work, or grasp the path the ball must fly. The novice plays the game, but he is unable to fully participate in it.

The blind golfer, like the novice, does not participate in the highest pleasures of golf. The blind or blindfolded golfer can play a good round of golf. He can hit a great shot, and even feel it in his hands. Nevertheless, he cannot fully visualize the shot he must make or watch the shot he hits. The pleasurable experience of the ball in flight, which mixes primordial, aesthetic, and emotional sensations, is denied him. Without the delightful direct imprint on his eye (our keenest sense) of the shot's flight, he can only vicariously experience the shot through the sensations in his hands and the descriptive words of others.

The highest pleasures of shotmaking depend on sight. The finest shots, however clever in conception, brilliant in execution, or rewarding in outcome, are not the most pleasurable, if their flight goes unobserved. Three different examples make this point.

In a night match at Hoylake in 1878, R. W. Brown—one of the game's early outstanding drivers—hit three unseen drives in a row. When the gallery located his third tee shot in the center of the fairway at the entrance of a rabbit's hole, they looked in the hole only to discover the player's two previous tee shots. These were three truly wonderful tee shots, but, their wonderful accuracy notwithstanding, these gorgeous shots flew unseen, and therefore unable to please, to their target.

In a second instance, the great British player Harry Vardon (whom many rank as equal to Jones as the game's greatest player) described one of the most remarkable shots of his entire career. On the eighteenth hole at Northwood, Vardon landed his tee shot two yards in front of the clubhouse. With only a short distance to the green and a thirty-foot building in front of him, he struck an almost perpendicular shot over the corner of the building that came to rest next to the pin. Even though Vardon knew almost immediately that he had hit a good shot, since the ball did not come careening back at him, his eyes did not participate in the shot's flight to its target and his soul was denied the pleasure of participation in its motion.

In a third case, Ed Tolley, a profoundly long driver who drove the 350-yard first hole at Troon in the 1923 British Open, played a brilliantly clever recovery shot. Tolley, according to Jerome Travis, found his hooked tee shot too close to the pricking prongs of a barbed wire fence (which marked out of bounds) to take a stance with anything more than a niblick. After much assessing, to the gallery's and his caddie's great surprise, Tolley took his long-shafted brassie from his bag and vaulted the fence. Leaning over as far as he could and from a very awkward position, he took a wonderful wrist swing. The shot he hit was straight and long and never stopped traveling until it trickled up on the green close to the cup. Tolley not only had the pleasure of thinking up a wonderfully clever shot, but he had the even greater sensual pleasure of watching its embodiment in flight and its successful conclusion. It carried with it yet another pleasure, as his shot permitted him to halve the hole in four.

A shot unseen is a shot not fully experienced. In the sensuous game of golf, the ecstasy of knowledge (as powerful as it can be) cannot rival the ecstasy of sight, as sight brings both participation and knowledge.

For this reason, shots into the sun and blind shots—long wood and iron shots around doglegs, over hills and obstacles, or even chips and putts where the ball cannot be seen from start to finish, or near finish—do not provide the same pleasure derived from shots seen in full flight. As satisfying as the craft of shotmaking is, it does not equal the ecstasy of the view of a shot in full flight. Even the satisfaction derived from the best-crafted bunker shots, long pitches, and putts can never match the pleasures of the eye following the full arc of the long shot.

Graceful Motion

The long shot rises and flies, drawing the eye upward to follow it. Its length adds to the duration the player spends in pleasurable, suspenseful, and anticipatory observation of his own creation. He sees its flight, towering in height or boring along on a lower trajectory, traversing a hazard, and landing on the green. In its flight the shot exceeds the time and space that measure it.

I wrote a poem following a flawless hole-in-one I made several years ago on the sixteenth hole of my home course.

> *My 160-yard eight iron flew the path of mind's eye.*
> *Only 25 yards out*
> *It found its arching way*
> *As it adjusted itself ever so slightly*

Into the slightest, rising fade.
From there on,
Its flight was pure and undaunted.

The flag, its polar star,
The cup, its magnet,
The ball held its course.
Until, with neither bounce, nor roll,
Neither hitting the pin, nor cutting the lip of the cup,
It entered the hole clean.
As if delivered by magic swing
And angelic intelligence.

Shots that fly high seem to belong, with all the prejudice of our eye's preference for skyward motion, to a higher and more sublime order of graceful motion.

During the shot's flight, the golfer leaves behind the common world of unclear thought, ambiguous emotions, constricted feelings, confused gestures, broken strides, half-formed steps, ungainly motions, and thick and sticky matter. The single good shot forms the primary unit of ecstatic delight in the garden of golf's pleasures.

*"To have achieved the greatest ambition . . . possible
for a golfer to aspire to, is in itself sufficient . . . to
prevent . . . any clear, distinct thoughts. . . . As
regards my feelings on that last green at Muirfield,
I can only say that I was dazed and unable to speak."*
—Harry Vardon on winning his first
British Open in 1896, My Golf Life

4

Magic Streaks

GOLF PRODUCES ANOTHER SORT of ecstasy—that of the
streak. It is not unique to golf, nor is it as pure as the ecstasy
of the wondrous shot. Because of its longer duration, it is
comprised of far more mixed pleasures, and is more de-
pendent on the thought and personality of the individual
player.

The ecstasy of the streak is often variously expressed as
"being on a run," "having it going," "being high," "being out
of one's mind," "being lucky," "being blessed," or "having the
gods smile on one." Even a good player cannot predict the
onset of a streak or merit its continuation and the rewards it
brings. The streak, at least at its outset, seems a matter of
chance, whose Latin root, *cadere*, means to fall, as if to fall out
of the sky. The streak of winning, in turn, is experienced as

continuing good luck, whose origin is the German word for happiness and good fortune, *Glück.*

The unexpected, subjective, and exalted state of the streak was expressed by Greg Norman after winning the 1993 British Open at Sandwich: "I hit every drive perfect. I hit every iron shot perfect. . . . I am not a person who boasts, but *I'm just in awe of myself* for the way I hit the golf ball today."

Of course, the streak takes different forms. For one player, it could simply be three or four good shots in a row; for a second, a succession of saving putts or chips producing good scores despite poor drives or second shots; for a third player, it could be an uninterrupted run of decent scores, like breaking 40 three or four nines in a row; and for a fourth player, it could be not missing a putt inside eight feet for two rounds. For the great Babe Zaharias, it was one of the fifteen straight tournament victories during 1946–1947. For Gene Sarazen it was to play the last 28 holes of the 1932 U.S. Open at Fresh Meadow in less than 100. Five-time British Open Champion J. H. Taylor's pitching was perfect in the 1894 Open. It was said that the only hazards he faced were the guide flags.

For Walter Travis, it was phenomenal putting that gave him victory, the first American victory, in the 1904 British Open. His magic touch seemed inseparable from the Schenectady putter borrowed on the tournament's eve. His run of putting was so phenomenal that in the course of one round, a fan, sensing that Travis was again on, began to bet anyone in the gallery in increasing amounts that Travis would sink the putt before him, be it 25 or even 35 feet. It didn't matter. By the final stages of the match, Travis's supporter had no one in the gallery to bet against, as his friends were broke and refused to bet any more against the hot American's putter.

In a piece called "The Mother of All Streaks," Don Jenkins wrote of Byron Nelson's play:

Most grown-ups of the golf persuasion are aware of the grandest streak in the history of the game. I speak of 1945, when Byron won 11 tournaments in a row and 18 for the year. What most grown-ups of the golf persuasion do not realize, however, is that Nelson's streak started in 1944 and ran through much of 1946. . . .

In '44, Nelson won eight of those 22 events, four in a row at one point, and was either first, second, or third in 17 out of the 22. His worst finish in '44 was tied for sixth at Oakland. Horrors. . . .

And what of 1946? Well, after all of the aforementioned, the constant pressure of trying to live up to everyone's expectations was burning a hole in what had always been a weak and unruly stomach anyhow. He went ahead and competed sporadically through the rest of '46, entering twenty-one tournaments in all. Guess what. He won six of them and even tied for the U.S. Open at Canterbury in Cleveland but lost by a slim one stroke to Lloyd Mangrum in what became a grueling 36-hole playoff.

The arithmetic for this amazing three-year period shows that Byron won 32 of the 72 tournaments he entered. That's very nearly half of them, folks. The arithmetic also shows that he was either first, second, or third in 57 out of the 72.

Naturally, the ecstasy of the streak need not require the legendary golf of a Nelson. Rather, it is the palpable perception by the player that he has somehow been raised beyond—perhaps extraordinarily beyond—his normal game. The streak can be a continuous run of good judgments or a succession of near-effortless decisions in shot and club selection. The sensation of a streak often involves the player's sense of body. Like any runner on a high, the golfer feels his body light, rhythmic, natural, and in the flow. The ecstasy contains an even fuller sensation of security and well-being for the player, who senses that he has been taken up by good fortune and is guided by a special charm or power. He feels he "has got it." His game is no longer his game. It is as if it has entered upon another season of play and into a different kingdom of the game: the difficult becomes easy; the impossible, possible. He need only see the shot and he hits it; he need only swing at the shot and it goes where it should go. No matter what trouble he gets into with his shot, he recovers and wins. He feels himself blessed, chosen to win.

Whatever the explanation, a streak is an exalted condition. When on a streak, the player feels as if he is not quite mortal, as if he is elevated beyond the doubts, hesitations, fears, and failures that normally haunt him. There is a surprising lightness to things. A new and immediate relationship seems to exist between him, his arms, swing, and the shot.

Even the more skeptical player can't explain away entirely his streak as merely a kind of mathematical necessity. He may argue rationally that the average of his game—or of any-thing—is invariably composed, not of average rounds, but by streaks beyond and below the average. However, this rationality pales before the powerful subjective experience of having been taken out of the world of the ordinary. And, of course, he faces the bafflement that all statisticians face in explaining why this streak is occurring now rather than at some other time.

Even the player who is reluctant to explain much by reference to good luck will find himself confessing his good fortune when caught up in a streak. After all, how does one explain the uncommon with the common? Explanations by opposites are rarely satisfying, at least to acute minds.

Throughout the history of golf, great and wondrous streaks have occurred. One tries and fails to explain them by the greatness of the athletes who carried them out for, invariably, streaks of such greatness and magnitude cannot be equalled in their momentous exceptionality. Take Lawson Little, for example, a player whom Herbert Warren Wind cites in a chapter titled, "The Man Who Could Play Matches," in *The Story of American Golf*. In the finals of the 1934 British Amateur at Prestwick, Little, coming off an important match victory at the Walker Cup, played the twenty-three holes it took him to defeat his final opponent "10 under 4s, with twelve 3s on his card." This set Little off and running, as he achieved a streak of victories no other player has neared. In 1934 and 1935, "he swept the British and American Amateur Championships in two consecutive years. No one else . . . has even come close to this historic double-double." To accomplish this, Little won thirty-one consecutive matches, many in an eighteen-hole format, where upsets abound. Wind attributes Little's success to his confidence, stamina, aggression, mercilessness when in the lead, and "contempt for breaks." Wind explains the wonder of Little's streak by the great wonder of his personality.

"The Grand Slam" and the Master of the Streaks

Amateur Bobby Jones invites the same sort of puzzlement. His streaks make him the quintessential player of the game. For instance, preparing for the 1928 Walker Cup, Jones, using woodshafted clubs, played a dozen rounds in a row below par: 69, 71, 69, 68, 68, 67, 68, 67, 70, 69, and 71. The number of victories he amassed between 1923 and 1929 is staggering and his Grand Slam victories in 1930, when he won the British Open and Amateur and the U.S. Open and Amateur, is singularly unrivaled in the annals of golf. Premising his discussion with the assertion that any player who wins more than one major championship is a truly great golfer, Wind records the phenomenal run of victories in Jones's short career. "Over eight years, Bobby won our National Amateur five times, our Open four times, the British Open three times, and the British Amateur once." In seven attempts at the U.S. Amateur between 1924 and 1930, he added one second to his five victories. In his eight attempts at the U.S. Open between 1923 and 1930, he added four seconds (two of which resulted from play-off losses) to his four wins. He won the British Open in three of his four attempts, even though it took him three attempts to win the British Amateur, which has seven rounds of 18 holes and a 36-hole final.

There is a magic about Jones's whole career. As early as 1926, Jerome Travis listed Jones at the top of his list of the game's six greatest players, ahead of Harry Vardon, Walter Hagen, J. H. Taylor, James Braid, and Macdonald Smith. Even Vardon himself, who was considered peerless in earlier times with his six wins in the British Open, wrote of Jones in his autobiography:

> *Even in the early days he made an impression on me. . . . [He] had the game at his finger tips. At the time I prophesied he would be one of the very best golfers ever seen. This year [1930] will go down in golfing history as Bobby Jones's year, as he seemed to win everything in which he competed. It would be impossible for anyone to accomplish more. . . . A patch of golf such as this lasts for a very short period.*

Jones's Grand Slam in 1930 is considered to be the greatest streak in golf history. Jones was playing better than ever at the start of the 1930 season. Jones himself thought that for a change he was hitting all his shots. One of his followers predicted, "He'll go to Britain and win the Amateur and the Open, and he'll come back here and win the Open and the

Amateur. He is playing too well to be stopped this year." On the eve of the last of his four victories, the American Amateur, the press, followed by a substantial part of the whole golfing world, was prophesying "the slam."

However, the start of the British Amateur at St. Andrews, the tournament Jones had never won, was characterized by several close scrapes. There seemed to be no inevitability about his victory. However, after taking nineteen holes to beat long-driving Tolley, a strange, inexplicable, and wonderful sense of invincibility settled on Jones, who, according to Wind, was by golfing disposition a confirmed fatalist. At critical points, Jones kept hitting the shot he needed to stay in or to win his match. He did this with what seemed "the certainty of a natural phenomenon." By the semi-final round, the feeling that Jones's triumph was mystically inevitable had communicated itself to many of the spectators. Even near the end of the round, when Jones was one down with three to go, a Scottish fan declared, "His luck is as fixed as the orbit of a planet. He cannot be beaten here." On the very next hole, his opponent drove his tee shot into a bunker and lost the hole. Jones glided through the final 36-hole round to a victory, about which the ecstatic Jones said, "I'd rather have won this tournament than any thing else in golf. I'm satisfied."

"No mysterious presence," Wind wrote, "walked hand in hand with Bobby Jones at the British Open at Hoylake." Jones struggled, worked for, and suffered his victory at this course, whose beginnings as a race track foretold its character of chance. Leading at the fourth round's start, Jones so badly bungled the par-five eighth, which he had birdied on the three preceding rounds, that golf critic Bernard Darwin suggested that a nice old lady with a croquet mallet could have saved him two strokes. Stunned by taking a seven after having been less than fifteen yards off the green in two, Jones recounted:

*As I walked to the ninth tee, I was in a daze. I realized
that in one brief span of only a moment or two, all the
efforts of the past three days had been just about washed
out. I wasn't looking at any Grand Slam, only at the one
championship. If ever a person could be made groggy by a
blow entailing no physical consequences, I had been made
so by that seven.*

Jones's confidence was broken. Stripped of the ecstatic
sense that he was chosen to win, he reverted to his fatalism:

[doing what] *nine out of ten people would do in similar
circumstances, I simply resolved to hit the ball as best I
could, to finish the round in an orderly fashion, if possible,
and let the result be what it would. I had no more thought
of attacking or defending or of being over par or under par,
but merely of finishing.*

Making it through the next five holes only two over par
helped Jones regroup for the five difficult finishing holes. He
made a brilliant and saving shot out of a bunker on the par-
five sixteenth with a massive concave sand wedge, a club
whose loft alone made the shot possible. The wedge had been
given to him the previous year by Horton Smith. It was a club
Jones rarely played. He had never before hit an important
shot with it. Jones made saving fours at the very difficult seventeenth and the testing eighteenth, assuring himself a two-
stroke victory.

While the idea of the emerging streak did not exempt Jones
from doubt, the whole golfing world espied the possibilities
of the Grand Slam. Jones returned from Britain to the cheers
of a whole nation eagerly awaiting the U.S. Open, the Grand
Slam's third leg, the next week at Interlaken in Minneapolis.

At the halfway point in the U.S. Open, Jones's score of 144 was in the company of several fine professionals, including Mac Smith, Armour, and Hagen. Jones accomplished on the third round his desire to shoot a round so low in score that his opponents would be demoralized. He played the front nine in 33; on the back, his bogey-bogey finish on the seventeenth and eighteenth holes did not stop him from shooting a stunning 35, highlighted by three pitches coming within inches of being sunk. Pursued by Mac Smith on the last day, Jones played an erratic round, mixing the beautiful and the ugly, for a 75. He sank a forty-foot putt on the eighteenth to claim a two-stroke victory.

Jones qualified for the U.S. Amateur, the last leg of the Grand Slam, at Philadelphia's Merion with a record-equaling 69-73-142. He coasted through the tournament. As if a great gate was compelled to open before him, his toughest competitors either failed to qualify or were beaten in early rounds by lesser players. Jones's opponents offered little resistance as he swept the National Amateur and achieved the Grand Slam.

Victory

With victory came other forms of happiness. First, there was the relief of being finished, free of the intense pressure that increasingly bore down on him during the season. He no longer had to suffer the dread of loss. He no longer had to undergo the ordeal of having to rally and to control his emotions— that fine edge on which every good tournament golfer must play. Jones, who the world pictured as serene, would even break down and cry after rounds as a result of the tension and exhaustion he experienced. There is then little wonder that Jones, who had announced to friends his intention of retiring from the game at the end of the year, kept his word. He had climbed the mountain to the top; thereafter, he would have been left playing in the shadow of his own greatness.

Jones stood forth as the greatest player of the game's entire history. He knew he had brought golf to another level.

Jones could survey his lifetime dedication to the game as having been worthwhile. He had experienced all the game's pleasures and ecstasies. He had seen putts run pure and smart across two breaks and sink as if destined by a higher force. He had seen putts enter the cup and circle the rim one whole time before they fell. And he had seen other putts wander and wobble, almost like drunks, seemingly crossing eternities of time, before they hesitated at the cup's rim, stopped, and then dropped in. He had the pleasure of other lucky shots as well—skulled irons arriving at their targets along the ground as if their failed flights were perfectly compensated for by their long rolls. And he experienced saving luck, as at St. Andrews's seventeenth ("The Wall Hole") on the last round of the 1930 British Amateur, when the gallery stopped his second shot from going beyond the green to the wall.

Jones also experienced those terrifying vigils that precede a difficult shot. He knew those nearly crushing contractions and dilations of time the player experiences as he takes the club back. And, like the toreador awaiting the bull's charge, he felt the mortal pause at the top of his swing. He knew golf's many "small eternities." He felt the flow of his body, the swish of his club, and the ascent of the ball, and he saw the shot climb and fly to his mind's preordained path. Jones had the conscious pleasure of knowing how well he had designed a shot and conceived a round. And he had the ecstasy of playing for one streak as no golfer has ever played. If anyone had come close to beating golf, he had.

"No kind of sport sooner finds out a man's weak point than does golf. . . . Golf demands the training of a lifetime. In golf this human machine of ours is put to the severest test; and if it has been overworked or abused, it is more than likely to break down between the teeing ground and the green."
—*Arnold Haultain,* **The Mystery of Golf**

5

Getting & Keeping the Grace

GOLF'S ESSENCE IS GRACE. Grace alone seems to account for glorious shots, wonderful streaks that run across a sequence of holes, a number of rounds, a season, and a whole career. Other orders of grace are those gifts that endow a player from birth—balance, rhythm, hand-eye coordination—and those strengths of character that define a golfer's play, such as intelligence, reflectiveness, equanimity, and pluck, a trait much admired by early British commentators on the game.

Given the many varied gifts required to become a good player, it is a puzzle why the majority of golfers make any effort to improve at all. It is a particular puzzle why golfers, especially those who have played the game for any length of time, don't abandon all hope that new clubs, tips, or practice can improve their game. Why don't they concede that they simply have what grace they have been given and accept their routine games? After all, golf—at least to some degree—does beat us all.

Every caddie knows the player's swing is as unalterable as his character. There is almost nothing the great majority of golfers can do about their swings. Those who hit from the top will hit from the top, as surely as those who quit at the ball will quit at the ball. Those who swing well on the practice tee, but speed up under pressure, will invariably do so on the course. Incorporating all possible tips and taking no end of lessons are of no avail, and the swing of the average player remains an unalterable endowment; the player's life will prove too short to improve on it.

Why golfers abide in the hope for improvement is a puzzle equal to that of why there is hope itself. One answer is the power of example of the exceptional player who somehow manages to improve his game over a long period, or the equally exceptional player whose game flourishes in middle-age as it never did before in his life. And there is even the rarer fellow who takes up the game in his late forties and by intelligence and persistence turns himself into a low-nineties or even high-eighties player within a couple of years.

A second answer to the puzzle about the golfer's hope is the belief that practice perfects. Jerome Travis's teacher, Aleck Smith, preached unrelenting practice.

If you want to learn to play golf, practice; and then after you have practiced for a while, practice some more. When you have practiced long and faithfully, and have your shots just where you want them, you'll find you are sitting on the top of the world if you observe just one little point—keep on practicing.

The aphorism "Practice makes perfect!" becomes a monstrous absurdity when applied to golf as it can rob players of years of their lives, result in trivial progress, and damage their characters. In fact there is evidence suggesting that if overdone, practice hurts players' swings and robs their concentration. Every player of the game knows how great the distance is from the practice range to the first tee. Even when the general case for practice is made (Jack Nicklaus once remarked that the more he practiced, the luckier he got), it is not clear that the value of practice applies to all players. Furthermore, practice is not easily defined. Surely it is not just simply a matter of sincere intention, hard work, and repetition. Instead, practice is an art. It requires the self-knowledge to work on what one most needs and the wisdom to accept the proper advice.

A third answer to the puzzle of a golfer's hopeful optimism belongs to our modern age's attitudes regarding the value of work, and the acceptance of self-help and new technology. This faith in improvement underlies modern democracy and industry. The surety of improvement is promoted by the growing legions of professionals, equipment manufacturers, golf schools and magazines that thrive on tips and optimism, just as medicine survives by promises of cures.

Already in 1914, Leach wrote in *The Happy Golfer* of the prolific new innovations in putters:

> *Hundreds of different putters have been invented. They have been made with very thin blades, and with thick slabs of metal, or other substances instead of blades. They have been made like spades, knives, like hammers, and like croquet mallets. . . . They have been made of wood, iron, aluminum, brass, gun-metal, silver, bone, and glass. Here in my room, I have the sad gift of the creator of a*

*forlorn and foolish hope. It is a so-called putter made in
the shape of a roller on ball bearings which is meant to be
wheeled along the green up to the ball. Like some others it
was illegal according to the rules. . . . And yet I once knew
a man who for a long period did some of the best putting
. . . with a little block of wood that had once served to keep
the door of his study ajar, to which had been attached a
stick that was made from a broom handle.*

In *Golfer at Large*, Charles Price wrote in the 1980s of
golf's "Gadgets and Gimmicks." He detailed a new inventory
of golf equipment.

*I have seen mink headcovers, bamboo shafts, concave sand
wedges, the twelve-wood, the seven-and-a-half iron,
floating balls, linoleum shoes, dome-shaped tees, distance
measurers, girdles that keep your elbows together, and an
iron that can be converted into everything from a two-iron
to a niblick, gadgets that steady your head, and putters as
ugly as Stillson wrenches.*

The Inner Side

In contrast to those golfers who pursue perfection with new
technologies, others seek it in the game's inner side. In his
classic work, *The Mystery of Golf*, Canadian Arnold Haultain
equated superiority in golf with the cultural history of its
birthplace, Scotland. He started from the premise that the
game required a mind "absolutely imperturbed and imper-
turbable." He believed that the puritanical Presbyterian Scots
came to the game admirably equipped. He believed particular

thanks were owed to their shorter Catechism, which left them with "a conscience void of offence both toward God and toward man." The Scot, Haultain argued, was captain of his own soul. He did not need to curb the ardor of his passions as players from the south would. Righteously confident and boldly independent, the Scot went about his affairs as successfully as his Calvinist counterpart, the Dutch businessman, carried out his commerce.

Another explanation for golfers believing in the possibility of perfection resides in the human assumption that we can do as we wish. We believe that we own our own bodies, and that they should do what we command them to do. Since we learned to walk and talk, we assumed (not entirely correctly, however) that our body is our first property and, ergo, our first slave. This assumption leads us to mistakenly conclude that we should be able to direct our body's actions during the few moments the golf swing takes place.

However, once the inherited presumption of body control is set aside, as it is for all serious golfers, a set of questions arises: Are there ways (indeed, ways too numerous to count!) in which we don't own and command our bodies? Don't we lack even a language which is full, elemental, and precise enough to talk to our bodies? Indeed, don't the parts and motions of the body form unexplored and uncontrollable dominions?

Surely the belief that we command our own bodies is at best a half truth. Let the American golfer who has gone to Scotland to play find a way, when stepping off the curb, to look right first rather than left. He will quickly discover that his body does not in all things yield itself to direct commands. Or, if I can issue one more directive to the reader, pick up your driver, and take the club back slowly and fully—hands, arms, shoulders, and hips—and then momentarily hesitate before starting all parts down at the same time. Some things are better left unthought for the sake of good play.

To the mistaken belief that we control our own bodies we join the false notion that we command our own minds. Since our minds are more intimate to us than our bodies, we mistakenly reason that they should be more responsive to our will. Our minds are least obedient when we are least confident. As any golfer knows, our minds are often least willing to listen when we order them most directly to do something. At such times they are like wild horses. Our attempts to herd them in one direction send them veering in the opposite direction. Every golfer has experienced the disobedience of his mind. Enlightenment for the golfer must be found in abandoning his quest to control his mind directly.

The desire for perfect control is also rooted in the desire to be blessed. Life moves forward on hope, as hope even fills minds from which belief and faith have long vanished. Hope—so common, so subtle—is, in the case of the golfer, identical to the folly which the great Dutch humanist Erasmus argued as inseparable from human life itself. Folly allows people to fall in love, to lend their energies to preposterous enterprises—and, in the case of the golfer, to pursue perfect golf. Folly also provides us with an inexhaustible source of delusions, such as the one that allows a hunter so in love with his hounds to imagine the scent of cinnamon in their droppings. Folly begets the golfer who thinks he will keep every drive on the fairway, hit every iron on the green, and sink all short putts.

Another source of the golfer's desire for perfection is his search for happiness. Like the person who has been invited into heaven, if only for a moment's stay, the golfer wants to hang on to the game's highest pleasures and repeat them as often as possible. Having once tasted the game's blessings (a truly great shot or a wonderful streak), the golfer—like the hunter or the fisherman who once bagged (or nearly bagged) the big one—will spare no expense in the effort to recapture the blessed moment. Once the golfer plays well, he is no longer content with average golf. He insists upon higher play. With the least sign of improved play, his desire is to have perfection upon command. He will rub every club before every shot to make its magic genie do his work. He will insist he have happiness by the mere wave of his magic niblick. One golfer at our club actually spoke to his clubs before he shot. When asked what he was doing, he replied, "Praying."

No golfer is so satisfied by a single shot or a great round that he will not wish for more. A little pleasure makes him greedy for more pleasures. The lover's passion is not quenched by a single embrace. The player wants his swing to be magic, so that it launches wonderful shot after wonderful shot. He wants course and tournament records to fall before him. Like the civilization that created him, he wishes to be able to have his pleasures at will.

The Requirement of Streaks

The golfer's search to hit good shot after good shot, however, has less mystical impulses. It arises simply from the game's requirement, which is not to hit a single shot, but to play a succession of fine holes—9 or 18, or, in a major tournament, as many as 72.

Every well-designed golf hole requires a sequence of shots. This is best observed on any good par four which, in contrast to par threes and par fives, is golf's most typical hole. A good par four demands a sequence of four good shots—a drive, a second shot, a chip and a putt, or two putts. Unlike par threes, par fours (as the matter of design) are not conceived to be dominated by a single tee shot. And unlike par fives, par fours tolerate fewer, if any, muffed shots. For instance, The Old Wall Hole at Troon, a 400-plus-yard par four, confronts the player with an angling boundary wall along the right side which increasingly squeezes the hole toward the left side, which itself is lined with a narrowing stand of unplayable gorse. The more distance the player tries to claim off the tee, the greater his chance of going out of bounds on the right or finding himself in the gorse on the left. Conversely, the more guarded his drive, the longer and riskier his second shot. The player has to play two fine shots to position himself for a makable putt for par.

Almost any good course has a hole or two that the player takes pleasure in parring, while great courses have sequences of three, four, and five holes that make par golf a great test and pleasure. For example, the Country Club of Detroit, where I caddied and which ranks in the top hundred clubs in the nation, has a strong succession of starting and finishing holes with no weak holes among them. The great Prestwick has three different sequences of wonderful holes: at the beginning, at the turn, and near the end. With any wind, these holes become a memorable test. Augusta's eleventh, twelfth, and thirteenth invite risk and threaten with water. Bearing the nickname "Amen Corner," the origin of which is unknown, these three holes often decide the winner of the Masters. Nelson once recorded three straight birdies to beat Hogan, and many years later, at age fifty-four, Hogan himself also made three straight birdies there. And in 1954, the wild and exhilirating amateur, Billy Joe Patton, muffed a chance to beat Hogan and win the Masters at "Amen Corner" by taking a disastrous double bogie on the par-five thirteenth, a hole where a birdie is almost imperative for winners of the tournament.

Like other athletes, the better golfer lives off runs and streaks. These include streaks of hitting no bad shots or shots that allow no recovery. The experienced player, however, recognizes the danger of letting a streak take him beyond his self-control. I remember the comment of an old Scottish caddie at Dornoch, the northern Scottish seaside course where the devil himself awaits to play you along gorse-lined fairways that lead to the immense and subtle greens where a whole separate game is played. The caddie poetically foretold the fate of his player who started off unusually well, "The bloom is on the rose too early." A streak of good shots—or even a single great shot—usually causes a player to get out of emotional control. Giddy from the heights to which the shot or the streak has propelled him, the player feels the need to descend to the ground below. Perhaps at some remote level of self, he believes that the vessel must be shattered by the excess grace it holds, that he must pay the gods back for the good he has received. Or, simply, struck by fear of the new terrain on which he finds himself, he hits bad shots to return to the familiar ground of the commonplace.

Professionals, too, get beyond themselves. Young professionals rarely win the tournaments they lead, and almost invariably follow a first tournament victory with a string of losses. Some play a good season or two, then disappear from the tour forever. Others win many tournaments over many seasons, yet on a major tournament's final day, they always manage to lose their lead. Like other golfers, they need grace and knowledge to win—not to be beaten by golf.

Grace or Control?

The golfer wants to play by grace and control. He wants to play beyond himself and, at the same time, to play within

himself. Our whole generation of the 1950s suffered this divided judgment of golf-as-grace and golf-as-control, and we
expressed adulation for our era's two best players, Hogan and
Snead.

We praised Hogan for—at least it seemed so to us—subdu-
ing the game by the force of his will. We read with reverence
his introductory masochistic proclamation in *Power Golf*
(1948):

> *I say that when you grip a golf club to take your first
> swing at a golf ball every natural instinct you have to
> accomplish this objective is wrong. Reverse every natural
> instinct you have and do just the opposite of what you are
> inclined to do and you will probably come very close to
> having a perfect golf swing.*

As much as we admired Hogan for his mechanical approach, our generation celebrated Snead for his natural swing.
We took to his easier approach to golf, which counseled at the
outset of his *How To Play Golf* (1946), "to err is human and it
is natural to do incorrectly the movements that are required
to swing the club successfully."

Earlier generations engaged in the same contradictory
praise. They glorified Robert Jones for his natural play, often
forgetting his strenuous years of youthful practice. At the
same time, they praised Walter Travis (the first American
player to triumph in the British Amateur after taking up golf
at age 35) for his self-made swing and calculated play. This
contradiction between grace and control was reiterated in the
decades following the 1950s. As some players were praised for
technique and control, others, like the young Arnold Palmer
and Seve Ballesteros, were truly loved for their inspired and
passionate style of play.

Palmer himself worried that golf had been given over to the graybeards of instruction who deny all the pleasure of "giving the ball a good healthy whack." In the introduction to *My Game and Yours* (1963), he argued (perhaps thinking of Hogan and Nelson, mechanical players who led the age of emerging specialists) that golf teachers:

> *have been lured into many complexities . . . people unfortunately do not take as naturally to swinging a golf stick, they usually have difficulties at the beginning that make them a gullible audience. . . . The game, therefore, lends itself to double-talk. We pros seem to be in possession of all sorts of occult secrets denied to mere common men. . . . I have seen golf books which were as difficult to read as advanced textbooks in physics, which they in fact somewhat resembled.*

The division between the player's conflicting views of golf as natural and mechanical is rooted in man himself. At one and the same time, the golfer wishes to play by grace and control. Simultaneously, he wants to play as an inspired artist and a cold-blooded accountant. His pleasure itself can be lost in his effort to satisfy these two opposing impulses. Try as he can, he finds it difficult to yield to a wisdom that teaches: Accept a world in which grace is given, work is required, and results cannot be determined.

*"Practice makes perfect, or as nearly as perfect as golf can be;
perfection makes assurance and concentration brings the mind
into coordination with the body. . . . There is no order of
relative importance. Each is as vital as the other."*
—*Jerome Travis,* **The Fifth Estate**

*"No matter how simple the correct golf stroke
ought to be, the job of describing it in language
everyone can understand is not so easy."*
—*Robert Jones,* **Bobby Jones on Golf**

6

Clubs, Swings, & Tips

THE GOLFER OF EARLIER TIMES assembled his bag of un-
matched, individually-made clubs one by one over a period of
years. If completed, this process of elimination provided him
with a playset of clubs that were deemed the ideal weapons to
do battle against bogey. He was not without superstitions
about these individual clubs and their powers and often gave
them names.

Representing earlier generations of players, Gene Sarazen's
autobiography shows him to be inseparable from certain
clubs. He mentions his well-known invention of the sand
wedge and his abiding affection for his jigger, a shorter,

shallow-bladed club with the loft of a mid-iron: "My old jigger was the most responsive club I ever owned." Sarazen tells
fellow players:

> Get on intimate terms with your clubs, so that none of
> them are strangers to you. Maybe you're carrying too
> many. I think a principal reason why we developed such
> solid shot-makers in the early days was that golfers played
> with only eight or nine clubs and got to know them all.
> When I won my third PGA title, I had five or six irons in
> my bag, no more. Any club that cut into my confidence I
> threw out. Whenever I pulled a club out during that
> tournament, I knew I was working with an old friend.
> "Here's an old fellow I know," I would feel as I gripped
> my mashie, for example. "I've had a lot of dealings with
> him. I can depend on this fellow."

During a recent golf telecast, Byron Nelson talked about
the six iron of his early days on the tour. It was called a spade
mashie then. He said he had a whole bag of shots with it—
ranging from an opened-face cut shot from 130 yards out, to a
closed-face low hook from three-iron distance. It was his favorite club, and he used it so much that the other pros began
calling him "Spade Nelson."

At my home course, Chandler Park, there was an older
player—perhaps he was in his early sixties but to us boys he
seemed ancient—we called "Captain Jigger." He drove,
played his mid-iron shots, chipped, and putted with his jigger.
He became our hero instantly and received his nickname
when he beat a pro with only his jigger. The driving-range
pro, having just finished tenth in the Michigan Open, showed
up at the course a few days later dressed to kill, and challenged that he would play the best ball of any two of us.
Stunned and intimidated, we stood mutely by when the old

man quietly replied to the pro, "I'll play you with one club alone, my jigger, for one hundred dollars. My only condition, I win all ties." The pro had left himself no room for retreat. He started off well and was three up at the end of four, winning the first, a long par four, and the third and fourth, par fives. He then lost the fifth through eleventh holes to Captain Jigger's successive pars for ties. A birdie at the par-five twelfth did little to save the pro, as Captain Jigger parred the thirteenth and fourteenth for a victory.

Many contemporary players annually change their clubs, like a ritual of purification and renewal. It is not uncommon to meet players who exchange individual clubs and sets of clubs throughout the playing season. After a poor round, disheartened players regularly stomp into the pro shop and buy a new set, as if this will end the curse upon them.

Ironically, yet gratefully, we called one of our members "Mr. Clubs." After nearly every round that he shot above his sixteen-handicap, he went directly from the eighteenth green, where he signed our caddie cards, to the pro shop. There he picked out a new club or two (usually a driver, often a putter, and occasionally a wedge) before joining his friends at the grill. More than once, an assistant pro told us, he even bought a putter or driver identical to the one he had traded in just months before. I remember once how he even left the driving range in the middle of a miserable practice session, only to return minutes later with a brand new set of clubs to finish hitting his bucket of balls. Frequently, the pro shop sold us the clubs he traded in. We were thankful to have them, even though for our first round or two, we superstitiously feared that they carried the curse of "Mr. Clubs." I even had one of his clubs regripped to remove his curse from the club.

Whether they regularly buy new clubs, or stick for decades with their old clubs, few golfers resist treating their clubs as magic wands. Even the most skeptical of golfers believes that some sort of special magic resides in his clubs. In any player's bag, he or she has one or two clubs that are really cherished (usually a driver, putter, wedge, or sand wedge, although sometimes it is the odd wood or iron). This favorite club, which may have been in his bag as long as he has played the game, has special powers for the player. It may have been given to him by his father; he may have won it as a youth in a skins game; he may have given it, in the home vise, an odd bend or twist years before; he may have won his first major victory with it; or, having developed a special trust for a club, like a putter or wedge used since childhood, he may be unable to conceive of playing without it.

Bobby Jones thought special powers resided in his "Calamity Jane" putter. Jim Braid, five-time British Open Champion, was identified with his brassie. There was the magic of Walter Travis's Schenectady putter, a center-shafted oddity borrowed on the very eve of his 1904 British Amateur victory. And most magic of all, for a single shot struck by it, was Gene Sarazen's four wood—a new model called the Turfrider, that had a hollowed-back sole—which he used to hole out his 235-yard second shot on the par-five fifteenth for a double-eagle two. Thus forcing a tie, he went on to win the tournament in a playoff. Wherever this four wood is now, it must still resonate with the powers of that shot made sixty-plus years ago.

When a player develops a special attachment to a club, he feels bonded to it like an old friend. He trusts it to do what no other club can do. He feels personally betrayed by it (or as if he has betrayed it) when he strikes a bad shot with it. The loss of such a cherished club by theft, by an unthinking and hurried trade, or losing it by carelessly forgetting it on the course, can damage a player's game, leaving him lacking in confidence until that particular club or its equal is found. More than one player traces his decline as a golfer to the loss of a club, especially his cherished putter. And there are cases of a recovered club being responsible for a recovered game.

Even though I have not yet come across a golfer's will in which he declares the disposition of his clubs, I am confident such wills must exist. Players don't want the wrong person to inherit their clubs, as if the wrong swing would betray the grace of his woods and irons. As concerned as the Japanese Samurai is about the proper transmission of his family sword, so the player wishes that his clubs pass into kindred hands.

If the player has clubs he trusts, he has other clubs of which he is wary. I had two such clubs, a nine iron I called "Shit Face" and a two iron I called "Mean-Son-of-a-Bitch." They were both capable of powerfully good and terribly bad shots. No club is as dangerous as a fickle one that can hit wonderful shot after wonderful shot, only to betray the player to disaster when he is most counting on the club. Sometimes a single heinous shot can totally destroy a player's relationship with a club, and the club will likely end its days rusting in a basement or garage, never to be played again.

Nicknames are common for favorite clubs. I, for instance, have christened as "Big Pete" an unidentifiable fifty year-old, fifteen-dollar, sand wedge. I know of no wedge as heavy, as good out of heather rough and seaside sand, and as capable of stopping a ball on the hardest surface. And I often talk to it, both before and after shots.

Every good player is in love with a club or two. I've read of a British champion who called his three clubs "Faith," "Hope," and "Charity." I recently met an old Royal North Devon player and clubmaker who told me to name every club in my bag. "Swing 'em and play to their name. That's the secret," he confided to me. "Take your time naming them," he continued. "Name them only when you know the best shots which fly from them." Then, as if in a trance, he took a club slowly from one of the many bags in his cluttered workshop and uttered the club's name. It was "Low Runner," I recollect, and he repeated "Low Runner" once softly in advance of his swing, again as he waved it over an imaginary ball, and then again as he gently stroked the club past the pretend ball. As he put the club gently back in the bag, he said, "Name it. Swing to its name." Then he added, "Your clubs must be your friends."

The Swing

As much as players count on favorite lucky clubs, hats, rituals, and amulets of one sort or another for their success, they understand that the good swing is the key to getting and keeping the grace. Faith in one's swing must be every player's first faith. With a good swing, one that the golfer can duplicate over and over, he can confront every shot as if he carries within him the most powerful magic. His swing can prevail no matter what situation arises. The player need only choose the right club, and either choke it down, alter the loft, and slightly alter the pace of his swing and length of his follow-through, and the rest will take care of itself. As if he were giving advice to meet life itself, an old caddie instructed his player, who was faced with hitting a long, high, faded three iron needing to clear a run of traps and roll up to the green between two rough-covered mounds: "Take the club back full, trust in God, and let it fly."

A swing of great rhythm is a matter of beauty, but any functionally sound swing that allows the golfer to play the game free of a war with himself greatly enhances the pleasure of the game. The good swing permits the player to enter the inner sanctum of golf's pleasures. He knows what it means to hit the ball solidly, crisply, delicately, and powerfully. He experiences his own body as good, and he delights in its unity and harmony. Grip, stance, address, backswing, downswing, impact, and follow-through become one. He senses his body, legs, and hands flowing together. Just as the dancer is joined to his music, so the golfer, at his best, is joined to the flow of his swing. Freed from errant impulses and instincts and from exaggerated and abrupt messages from mind to body, the player can let his body perform what his eye has seen.

The good swing is the holy grail of golf. To attain it, golfers practice, take lessons, lose their jobs, leave their families, and humble themselves by groveling before endless, useless, and stupid tips. In bathrooms, on airplanes, and in the waiting rooms of barber shops and trust departments of banks, the golf addict scours golf magazines for tips as precious as rare gems. Especially in the dead of winter, for example, the golfer ponders his swing's improvement.

Reason does not deflect the ardent golfer from believing that he can attain the coveted grooved swing. In his most desperate condition, the golfer loses his immunity to the most irrational ideas.

I remember when our assistant club professional, Ralph Yanqui, called my friend Ron Helveston and I from behind the caddie shack over to the driving range to watch him hit what he called his new wonder shots. "I've got it," he declared, and then proceeded to hit several shots with his seven iron. While they looked like the normal low-flying, slightly fat sevens he usually hit, he declared each shot to be more glorious than the preceding one. He explained that by reverting from the Vardon overlap grip to a baseball grip, the shots he struck were not flying with backspin, but were actually spinning like bullets. I jeered at his declaration, instinctively suspicious of anyone who claimed he "had it," and I also didn't believe that even Ralph Yanqui could change the laws of physics. My friend Ron, more docile than I and zealous of attention, accepted Ralph's new-found secret. Ron saw Ralph's shots spinning like bullets, while I laughed. Ron was rewarded by being allowed to hit balls with Ralph on the range. Ralph added to my punishment: "One day Ron will be on the tour, and you won't." A few days later, I noted that both he and Ron had quietly reverted to the Vardon overlap grip, and I never heard again of golf balls spinning like bullets.

Every player of the game knows a fellow player who is a gnostic: someone who believes the key to the game is locked in its secrets. Bobby Jones's father was such a gnostic. No sooner would Bobby report to his father's law firm than his father, a dedicated golfer, would beckon him through the connecting office door to show him "something I discovered the other day," and ask Bobby for his opinion. Bobby commented that his father "always seemed to think he was on the verge of discovering the secret of the game. It cost him untold agony, but he loved it. The secret he had shown me in the morning never worked in the afternoon, but he always discovered a new one on the seventeenth hole and went home happy and with something to show me next morning."

Jones himself worked through hundreds of golf tips. Many were simple and modest: Mentally prepare yourself to play golf before you start out; practice before you play; don't rush to the first tee; swing within yourself during the first few holes. Other tips were subtler. For instance, the putt that has the greatest chance of sinking is the putt that dies at the hole, for it can use the whole cup; whereas the putt that is hit firmly must hit the back of cup to go in and, if missed, may leave you with a long putt back.

Some tips became the basic elements of his swing and he claimed that they were keys to all good swings. For instance,

Jones taught that a full pivot should be taken off the ball and that the left side should not be stopped prematurely on the downswing. At some point in the backswing, Jones specifically instructed, the player must pick up his club and take it fully back. Jones concluded a chapter on instructions:

> *Swinging the clubhead back in a flattened arc around the knees, . . . makes it inevitable that the striking motion should become a rolling or a pushing action. The proper stroke, if I may say so, is a slicing action which does not slice across the line of play, but sends his club straight through the ball on the line to the hole.*

Tips about the swing abound. One recent book has for part of its title, "Over a Hundred Secrets of the Big-money Pros." For nearly a century, there has been a growing swell of golf instructional literature. With a lot of text and a few photos, or a lot of photos and little text, they depict the swing as a set of steps from address to follow-through, which are to be learned step by step from start to finish. They imply that the swing, a matter of flow and rhythm, can be cut into pieces like so many still photographs. Some of these books aim at power (they usually stress a large leg and shoulder turn), while others stress rhythm and flow by concentrating on the fullness and pace of the swing. Some spend a lot of time on grip and set-up, while others spend time on take-away and position at the top of the backswing. As suggested earlier, some texts stress the natural swing, while others, like those by Hogan and Nicklaus, preach the methodical swing. The novice can emerge from an encounter with all the riches of these suggestions impoverished of all instincts—no longer certain (and painfully befuddled) whether he should meet, stroke, sweep, or hit the ball.

Some basic teaching texts strive for simplicity. My favorite is Byron Nelson's primer. It was the first golf book I read. Long on photographs and short on explanation, it appealed to my youthful taste. Aside from a few essentials on grip and address, it proposes a slight alteration of stance (from open to closed) as one goes from nine iron to driver. Other texts have embedded in them the player's own favorite tips, even though they did little more than justify the commercial venture of publishing a text. For example, I believe that Hogan's technique of the extreme pronation of his wrists set back a whole generation of good players. And I would guess that Tommy Armour's insistence that at the last moment one hit as hard as one can with one's right hand accounted for innumerable out-of-bounds shots wherever his book was read.

All tips about the swing finally betray the golfer and rob him of both his swing and any pleasure he might experience, unless frustration is, as there is some reason to believe, his secret delight. Advice about the swing fails for a variety of reasons. The most obvious reason is found in the differences between human bodies. Proportions, muscles, and rhythms vary from player to player, and so must good swings. Recognizing this, the great Harry Vardon said that everyone should choose his own putting style and that even the best putters (among whom the older Vardon surely did not number) should not be imitated. Vardon even suggested that humans are like the capricious clock that, when turned on its side, ticks well. His concluding advice was even more humbling: that often great improvements have been made in a player's putting results when an accidental hand injury causes the player to grip the club less tightly. Vardon himself experienced that the defiant short putt (when perhaps eye and body are too close to the cup to aim) has defeated the greatest golfers.

A second reason why tips about the swing are suspect is that golf requires more than one stroke. A swing that is good

for one shot may, indeed, not be good for another. Even if a
player has one essential swing, he makes a different stroke
with his woods and irons—the shots he sweeps and the ones
he hits. There is a significant difference between driving off a
tee and playing a fairway wood off a tight lie; between keeping a long iron low and sending one high and fading; between
a punched and a full iron; or between a soft and fluffed pitch
and one hit low, with a lot of backspin.

Swings have varied throughout the history of the game to
accommodate changing styles, conditions, and technologies.
Early golfers needed a longer, fuller, and more patient swing
to account for the torque of the wood shaft of the older clubs,
while modern players, in possession of metal or composite-
material shafts, can slash at the ball. Confronted by heavy
winds, traditional seaside players, needing to keep shots
down, found the draw hook the preferable shot. Modern
players, by contrast, who fire shots over obstacles at greens
that take backspin are more likely to prefer high, faded shots,
especially from their mid-irons down.

In the December 1992 issue of *Golf Illustrated*, Johnny
Miller claimed to have distinguished between two different
swings: that of his and Nicklaus's generation of the '60s and
'70s, and that of newer players. The older swing, which he
calls "the reverse C" (describing the player's body at impact
with the ball), relied on driving legs and had a fixed center;
whereas the modern swing, which moves weight and head off
the ball to the right side, is flatter and depends for its accelera-
tion on returning the body to the ball and onto the left side
that more quickly straightens and turns.

Beyond differences in swings, golf tips usually go awry for
other and more subtle reasons. There is, first of all, a set of
problems involved with language: How well can language describe the golf swing, and, even to the degree it is successful,
how well does the body understand and accept a logic of

command. Talking to one's body is an art, an art of no complete masters. It must be recognized that bodies, like minds, have moods; they can be keen or groggy, gentle or aggressive, nervous or relaxed. Some days the parts of a player's body are in harmony, while other days, hands, eyes, and legs behave like strangers to each other. Bodies often need hours to be taught the simplest golf instructions, and, if learned at all, they are often promptly forgotten on the course. In contrast to bodies at rest, bodies in motion are particularly adverse to instruction. Anything other than the gentlest and simplest message will set them in open rebellion. Defiantly, they jerk, stop, and do the opposite of what they are commanded during the two seconds of the backswing and the one second interval of the downswing.

As Harvey Penick points out, we talk to our bodies in the wrong way. For instance, such commonplace advice as hitting through might lead the player to the serious error of getting his body beyond the ball. And often in telling the body to do one thing, it stops doing something else. For example (I think of my own woes), the golfer tells himself to take the club straight back in one piece. The result (often after a few successes) is that, though he now moves his club back correctly with his hands, he stops pivoting the rest of his body back. Or, adopting another tip (one that I got from Ray Milan at our country club), the golfer is told he should set his left knee on his downswing. Even though this advice works wonderfully for a shot or two, or even for four or five shots, he soon finds his knee so far in advance of his downswing that it is precipitating his downswing, stifling his backswing, denying all movement to the left side, and causing a hideous jerking stop at the swing's bottom.

The golfer seeks the good swing in a fixed number of mechanics (call them fundamentals) such as a good grip, weight transfer, and a point of pivot on the way back and through.

He seeks to groove them. However, in the end, even mechanics betray him, as they can rigidify his muscles (which Vardon conceived to be the worst of things that could happen on fairway and green).

Even concentration can be bad, if it turns into tension, which shortens the swing and robs its rhythm. As Bobby Jones pointed out (his father was the example he had in mind), "the player's practice swing is almost always far better than that made with the intent of striking the ball." In his practice swing the player, Jones explained, is at ease; whereas when he swings at the ball he has adopted a strained and unnatural posture. It is the frills of the actual stroke, he explains, that distort the simpler and more rhythmic practice swing.

The golfer's attempt to make the game's pleasure his own by the direct control of his swing leads him to introduce awareness precisely where it doesn't belong. Like the lover who destroys his relationship with his beloved by too much talk and too little action, the golfer wrecks his swing when he introduces more conscious directions than his body can carry out, as only infinitesimal bits of time exist between moments of the swing. As in love, the body should be allowed to enter the flow of things.

Of course, the tips of others are often as dangerous to one's game as are the player's own set of tips. A North Dakota pro taught my fifteen-year-old daughter to recock her wrists at the top of her swing, which started her hitting the ball from the top of her swing. Some many years later, she still has not overcome this error which stole the predictable draw hook that had enabled her to win a series of tournaments.

My friend, Don Olsen, goes even further in his indictment of professionals and their tips. He wrote me:

I think most pros do far more damage than improvement. Judging from my own experience and knowledge, I always

found those how-to articles in golf magazines to be
misleading at best and often wrong. Gary Player used to
make comments that would drive me up the wall. You
shouldn't be thinking about anything when you hit the
ball. One pro I knew never saw a swing he wouldn't
change. He wanted to turn everyone into Ben Hogan. . . .

I think it is possible to teach alignment of the stance, ball
position in the stance and short game technique to a certain
extent and also to teach how to read a green properly and
determine the line on which to putt and certain putting
strategies. But as to the swing itself, the only way to teach is
by imitation. The pupil tries to mimic the professional
swing. That's the most, and best, that can be done.

Practice Talking to Yourself

The practice ground is where the golfer courts his body. If the
golfer wishes results, he must work patiently as he tries out
new approaches, refreshes himself on old lessons, and develops an ever more subtle conversation between his mind and
body. In the course of this conversation, he remembers old
advice, rejects some new ideas as being unfit for his body, and
modifies other suggestions at his body's insistence. Learning
what doesn't work is worthy information to be gained on the
range. Finally, the player's conversation with his own body
must reach down to the movement of his muscles and his
bodily sense of rhythm and flow. Hence, this conversation
reaches levels that contemporary psychology and physiology
fail to reach.

In the same previously-quoted letter, Don Olsen told me
the practice field is his "dream world." He also explained the
therapy he finds for practice:

*I always like practice as much as play. It takes me into
another world. When I go out in front of the house to hit
my plastic ball, it's like a visit to a great therapist, only
cheaper. Plastic balls (the dimpled kind) are $1.79 a
dozen. . . . A dozen balls will last a month.*

Don went on to describe how Ellsworth Vines, a tennis star
in the the 1930s, built his entire golf game on the practice
course before he ever set foot on the tournament course.

[He] *took up golf with an eye to becoming a professional
golfer. It was said that he did not actually play a course for
a year (or was it two years) but stayed at the practice range
and learned to hit all the shots. That's all he did for a year
or two was practice. He learned to putt, chip and pitch and
hit sand shots and hooks and slices. Finally, he was ready to
actually play a golf course and it is said that he went out
and shot around par the very first time he played. A nice
story. Must be a lesson in there somewhere.*

Of course, few players approached the game like Vines or
old man Travis. Most players are no more graced in their golfing self-discourse than individuals are in identifying their own
pleasure and directly pursuing it. It is not accidental that, with
notable exceptions, the great golfers began the game when
they were young, either as caddies or, like Jones, as members
of a golf club. Then they had time and, like the tongues in
their mouths, their bodies were supple and free of a lifetime of
inhibiting instruction. They were able to learn quickly this
new language of mind and body. Quick to imitate and not
afraid to dare, young players are able to blend (as adults rarely
can) imitation and naturalness into what J. Gordon McPher-
son, in his *Golf and Golfers* (1891), called an "individuality of

style which can be regulated, but which can never be obliterated after it has been found."

While all players want to keep the grace, many want to do so without practice. Practice for them is a painful duty. They do not understand practice as the means to bring mind and body into harmony. Nor do they lend credence to the subtle advice that practice is a way to hit fewer poor shots. After all, as Jones saw the essence of his own mature game, golf is not about singular great shots; rather, it is about the quality of the player's average shots. Discounting putts, all but a handful of shots in a round are flawed in one way or another. Jones quoted one wit who stated that, "No man has mastered golf until he has realized that his good shots are accidents and his bad shots good exercise." Or, stated differently, practice is a way to get shots closer to the center of the clubface. Yet, Jones also wrote, "The secret of beneficial practice is keeping a definite idea upon which to work. If you cannot think of some kink to iron out or some fault to correct, don't go out. And, if there is a kink or fault, as soon as it has been found and cured, stop immediately and don't take the risk of unearthing a new one or exaggerating the cure until it becomes a blemish itself."

There have been outstanding players who enjoyed practice more than play. One such player was Harold Hilton, British Amateur champion four times. His last victory came in 1913, on the eve of World War One. In his chapter "Practice—The Foundation of Excellence," in *Modern Golf* (1922), Hilton argued that players are made rather than born. He confessed after decades of golf to still "enjoying to this day an hour all alone by myself on the links more than the pleasure of participating in the most interesting and pleasant match one can imagine." The great woman golfer, Mickey Wright, agreed: "I have no interest in translating my name into a million dollars, or any amount. To me golf means one thing and always has: the pure pleasure I get from swinging a golf club."

Tips, Tips, & More Tips

Like the advice we receive to make and keep ourselves happy, golf tips are as numerous as they are fruitless. Indeed, some tips are just downright silly; for instance, one classic golf instructional book instructs the player simultaneously to think of himself in a barrel for his hip turn, while conceiving of his shoulder turning up and down. Another tip that I received suggests that the player conceive of the swing as fundamentally a pitching motion of the right hand. This tip helped my hook not one bit.

Tips have been supplemented by a host of commercial gadgets such as hoops, rings, ropes and, most recently, shafts that break in two if the club is improperly taken back.

Tips are golf's common currency. "Slow back," "head down," and "down and through," count among the games most common clichés. And, as in all things, there are a certain number of golfers who enjoy giving other players tips. One public links player I knew told every player he played with, "At the top of your backswing point the shaft of your club straight at the target." It didn't matter if he was advising a twelve-year old playing for the first time, or a seventy-year-old with severe arthritis. Advanced players manage their swing with such tips as, "straight back for a foot, then up"; "hesitate at the top"; "move a firm left wrist through to the target." A hooker, who might hook for half-dozen reasons, including his body shape, will have a long inventory of tips: "get the weight back on a steady right knee"; "get the club back and up"; "start downswing with gentle move of the left hip toward the target and keep on going through"; "keep left knee bent"; "stay behind the ball."

Unfortunately, even the simplest tips mutate themselves in the course of a round. A tip that starts out being useful often ends up producing the most unwanted consequences. It becomes exaggerated, or, like so many of our medicines, mixes poorly with other tips. Such seemingly safe tips as staying down through the shot, or keeping the left foot planted on the downswing can result in stopping the player's flow through the ball. Or a tip can produce a good thing for one part of the player's game—say, for instance, his driving—and worse things for other parts. Part of the genius of Nicklaus's game has been explained by his ability to make slight adjustments in his swing during a round.

Changing course conditions likewise change the tips that key the players' games. For instance, strong winds, as a young Scottish professional explained to me, tend to make the hooker's hook worse. Winds tend to make the player hunch over. Consequently, he flattens his plane and shortens his backswing, which leads the player to further abbreviate and flatten his swing, resulting in yet greater hooking. The seaside hooker's tip then must be: "Don't be afraid of the wind—stand up to it, and swing full into it."

Tips, however subtle, are insufficient even for a good player when his game turns sour. Even a few bad shots can make a player desperate for a saving tip. Like the addicted drinker's need for his bottle, he needs a tip to survive the round. With each bad shot, the desperate player imposes upon himself a new order of instructions. His advice has the effect of making him a frightful mess of disjointed consciousness and erratic motion. He ceases to perceive the shot he must hit. He converses futilely with himself. He endeavors to make his swing into precisely what it cannot be: a matter of conscious command.

The only hope of the desperate player—at least I have found this to be my only hope when I am desperate—is the following advice: "Shut up the voices inside yourself as best you can. Put away all tips and directive ideas. Have a clearly defined target." (Penick told his pupils "to take dead aim.") Look at the back of the ball, and take your club back fully and slowly, which was something Jones advised all players to do, especially during the closing holes of any match, when pressure speeds up the swing. Finally, start down gently, and just trust in what happens. In the end, every player must surrender himself to the graces of his eye and swing.

Over the course of time, the good player will necessarily work his way through many tips. He will discard some tips, incorporate others, and make variations and combinations of yet others. In the end, he will discover that no one tip will singularly assure his swing a sustaining grace. He will recognize that no one tip saves a swing or elevates a player beyond his game. Rather, he will use a variety of tips about fundamentals (grip, stance, backswing, and position at top) and shots (draws, fades, uphill and downhill lies, etc.) to inventory his swing on the practice range and to provide his swing some gentle guides for actual play. Beyond that, what he needs to play is a general attitude that strikes a balance between the enduring and mutable qualities of his swing.

I remember one day as a boy, on a loop caddying for four of the club's better but older players, how they openly argued about the secret of the game. Struggling with my own swing, I listened as earnestly as if I had been invited to the School of Athens. My favorite player of the loop, because he was the most friendly and generous of the four, argued that the essence of good golf was to hit through whenever possible, and to turn a slight draw whenever possible. His partner contended that to play well you must put your body in every shot, chips and putts included. The third contended that only when you see a shot, can you hit it. The fourth said that the essence of golf is, "Swing gracefully, play your shots one at a

time, and don't be mean to yourself." In retrospect, I consider
their tips as good as any I was ever to hear.

Nevertheless, no advice can precede the recognition that
golf is a game to be played, not a thing to be possessed. By
playing golf, the golfer agrees to develop skills (which can
never be fully perfected) and to play in a domain where
chance, luck, and grace have a place. The bad is always possible. Even though there are moments when the player knows
with uncommon clarity and prescience that he will hit a good
shot or sink a long putt, the outcomes of shots, rounds,
matches, and tournaments are always far more in doubt than
they are certain. Disaster itself lurks in a misthought shot, on
any particular patch of ground, and in the gusting wind.
However much the golfer practices or however long he has
played, the swing remains a delicate and shifting mix of balance, coordination, sequence, and rhythm. It is like the most
ethereal of elements. And if all this were not the case, golf
would not be a game, and would be less the art and the play
that it is.

The golfer who wishes to delight in the game must play the
game with a certain equanimity about its pleasures and pains.
The golfer must arrive on the first tee with the good faith of
intending to shoot well. But once out on the course, he can
only do the best he can. He can only let his shots fly as they
will. He cannot presume that grace will be with him. He cannot command his pleasures and ecstasies. Like the fruits of
love and friendship, the goods of golf are not secured by will,
nor are they free of pain.

"Golf is an awful game."
—*Harry Vardon, from Henry Leach,* **The Happy Golfer**

"Golf is a humbling game."
—*George Low*

"Golf is the refined modern equivalent
of the ancient barbarous Ordeal."
—*Arnold Haultain,* **The Mystery of Golf**

7

Pains

GOLF IS A MEAN AND CRUEL GAME, as it affords so many
ways to make errors. We must agree with Robert Hunter
when he says, "Golf beats us all, and that is the reason we
shall never cease loving her."

The forms of golf's pains are as multiple and varied as its
pleasures. They can be as immediate and indisputable as a
topped, duck-hooked, or banana-sliced drive; an iron shot
that is skulled, chunked, or shanked; a double-hit pitch; or, a
stabbed, scuffed, or pushed putt. Each of these shots is experienced as immediately awful to the hands, ugly to the eyes, and
deserving of the disdain of others. Only rarely are the consequences of these shots any less bad than their sensation. And

even when their outcome is favorable, the player still experiences them as an insult to his skill.

The horizon of golf's pains also includes a range of misfortunes or disasters. These pains, so immediately and strongly felt, play themselves out over a long period on the inner shores of the player's spirit where they differentiate themselves into the many forms human hurt takes.

Many of golf's pains are as subtle as the human spirit itself. For instance, the golfer plays well; his shots fly high and straight; he wins the adulation of others; yet, inwardly, a voice painfully reminds him that he doesn't play well enough to be as good as he wishes or to justify the time he invests in the game. Inwardly, he regrets his dedication to the game.

Places of Pain

Testifying to the place of pain in golf, individual shots, stretches of holes, and courses themselves are inextricably linked to disasters and to the destruction of individual players. On great courses, individual holes, bunkers, and other hazards are commonly named after the player they defeated. On the Royal St. George, with holes called "The Kitchen" and another "The Suez Canal," there is a bunker called "Kite's Grave," where Tom Kite blew his two-stroke lead on the final day of the 1985 British Open by landing in one bunker and then playing into another. And there is a more famous indentation on the course called "Duncan's Hollow." Having played a wonderful underpar last round in the 1922 Open in the teeth of awful weather, Duncan still needed a par four on the eighteenth to tie Walter Hagen. Instead, Duncan, who was lying two just off the green in that small hollow, scuffed his mashie chip shot. He left it fifteen feet short of the cup. He then missed the putt and lost the tournament, though finishing with a 69 and one of the greatest rounds ever played at the Royal St. George.

Robert Hunter (whose *Links* was the first book published on golf-course design in the United States) believed that St. Andrews is the most defiant of golf's great courses. Despite the many defects he attributed to the course—its many parallel holes, shared fairways, and shared greens—he could not restrain expressing his respect for it: "St. Andrews should be the one and only course which stands above and scorns all criticism. There is something in the very terrain that outwits us. . . . We never have a sufficient variety of shots or quite enough skill and accuracy to play St. Andrews as we should like to play it. That is," he concluded, "what gives the old course its *enduring vitality*. It is the most captivating and unfair, the most tantalizing and bewitching of all courses."

The long par-four seventeenth, the Road Hole, is the most infamous of St. Andrews's holes. It has broken as many hearts and stolen as many championships as any closing hole in all of golfdom. It was here that Tom Watson's three-iron shot, from 195 yards, failed to hold the green and ended up next to the stone wall, costing him the 1984 British Open. Here, also, Tommy Nakajima lost the Open in 1978. He hit the green in regulation, but then putted off the green into the cavernous Road Bunker on the left side of the green. He took four shots to get out of it before he got his nine on the hole. In the process of his defeat, he renamed the bunker itself, now called "The Sands of Nakajima." Nakajima and Watson were two recent victims of the Old Road Hole. In the 1885 Open, David Syton, an outstanding St. Andrews amateur, squandered a five-shot lead on the last round by going back and forth between bunker and road for an eleven.

While the old course at St. Andrews is strewn with heartbreaks, golf critic Bernard Darwin believed that Prestwick has been "the scene of more disasters that have passed into history than any other course. The Road Hole at St. Andrews [the seventeenth] may possibly hold the individual record, but surely Prestwick comes first in point of collective deviltry." Darwin described how a half dozen of Prestwick's holes had brought Britain's greatest golfers (Braid, Hilton, Taylor, and Park) to their knees. At the end of his recitation of the litany of suffering caused by Scotland's greatest field of woe, Darwin went on to confess that he thought his knowledge of Prestwick's mischievous holes and bunkers was complete until he examined an old map of the course. He was "aghast" to discover that he had never heard of such disaster sites as the "Grave of Willie Campbell," the "Slough of Despond," "Purgatory," the "Precentor's Desk," "Tom's Bunker," and "Sandy Neuk," all of which were already named on a map of the course's original twelve holes.

However, one does not need an esoteric demonology to name the main devils that exist at Prestwick, St. Andrews, and other great links courses. Instead, they have common names—wind, sand, contour, and undulation. Robert Hunter remarked, "The charm of the seaside courses of Great Britain lies in their multi-formity, their unconventionality, their infinite variety." The consequences of his main argument are that, "good golf is the product of a good course, there can be no real golf without hazards, and unless these be varied, plentiful and adroitly placed there will be no great golfers." Hazards, of course, mean pain and disaster.

Stories of Pain

In golf, as in life itself, players tend to forget disasters, remembering instead the good and glorious days. Players trick themselves into forgetting how much their pleasures of golf

were purchased by pains. Even though everyone who knows
the game knows stories of wasted lives, golf's official memories (those supported by its associations' museums and displays in clubhouses) are dedicated to recording victories
rather than detailing the defeats and inventorying the disasters
and the broken lives that went with them.

One such tragic life was that of now long-forgotten Johny
McDermott, the son of a Philadelphia mailman. At nineteen,
he won the U.S. Open in 1911 and repeated in 1912. McDermott sacrificed his life to golf. He compensated for his small
stature with awesome accuracy. As Gerard Astor wrote, Mc-
Dermott practiced hitting irons onto a tarp he spread out on
the fairway as his target. As his technique improved, he substituted a newspaper for the tarp. His intention was to be the
world's best player of the game. Set on teaching the Brits their
own game, McDermott went to the 1912 British Open. He
shot an astronomical 96 and failed even to qualify. McDermott returned to Hoylake for the 1913 Open. His final round
83 "ballooned his total to 315, good enough for a fifth place
finish, best ever by an American, but eleven strokes off the
pace set by J. H. Taylor."

After that, things went downhill for McDermott. He was
plagued by financial reversals. His derogatory remarks about
visiting British players got him chastised by the American
golf community. His chance to revenge himself in the coveted
Open in 1914 was lost, not by play, but when he missed a
ferry on the way to the tournament and was disqualified. On
the way home, his ship collided with another ship and he was
forced to escape in a life boat. The fires that once burned so
brightly in McDermott were extinguished. Thereafter, he entered into "a steep emotional decline and at only twenty-three
years of age entered into a life of rest homes and sanitariums
where he stayed until he died when he was eighty."

McDermott was one of the countless many whose fortunes in golf ended, as they can in any competitive venture, in pain and defeat. Herbert Wind surveyed this pain with this truism: *"Whenever there are winners, there must be losers."* "The unpredictability of the game," he continued, "is one of its bittersweet charms, and in the end the breaks even up fairly well." But then, as if to contradict his airy abstractions with real living examples, he went on to describe three players—Macdonald Smith, Leo Diegel, and Harry Cooper—who played some of the very best golf of the interwar years and for whom the breaks somehow didn't even out fairly. They won tournaments galore and huge percentages of prize money and their exquisite shot-making equaled the best, yet their great successes became an occasion to speak of men, Wind wrote, "who are remembered not as winners but as losers. Season after season, one of the three was always on the brink of a victory in a national championship, but they always found a way to lose." As is true of many contemporary players, their misfortune was that they were called to win everything in the game but its great championships.

Golf fans often remember pain, hurt, disaster, and failure best. They called the great Sam Snead the player who couldn't win the PGA. It took recent victories in major tournaments by Greg Norman and Tom Kite to free them from being defined as second-place finishers, though Norman's more recent final round collapse at the 1996 Masters puts him in a special category in contemporary times.

Golfers forget that there is more losing than winning in golf. Forgetting serves the hope we cherish and lets us get on with the folly of trying to move a ball flawlessly, shot after shot, around a course for the sake of the game and glory. The golfer, however miserable his game, is continually renewed by hope, as any new idea about the swing or type of club sends the worst hacker to the first tee full of expectations.

Golfers pour their whole soul into visions of what they intend to do with a single swipe of a club. And when things go wrong, they suffer bitter disappointments. They treat their illusions as near certain possibilities and their defeats as unlikely occurrences. A golfer can become a pitiful creature if his putting goes bad. A golfer's wife on a flight from Scotland with my son and me confided that she found it easier to live with her par-shooting husband, a commodity broker, in bad times on the market than when his putting was bad.

Some golf pains are simply bizarre. They can hardly be considered tragedies, even by the most avid golf fans. Disasters, as every student of tragedy has been taught, can be too redundant or grotesque to elicit anything other than hilarity. When players (professionals at that!) whiff a ball thrice, or make a 9, 10, 11, 12, or 13, there is insufficient nobility for the compassion tragedy requires. What else is it, if not a farce, when a young professional at the 1978 French Open shanked enough balls out of bounds on the par-five thirteenth to make a 21? Tommy Armour reported a 22 on a single hole in the 1927 Shawnee Open.

None of these rival, according to Jerome Travis, this story from Pennsylvania,

> . . . *From the tee of the Binnekill Water the woman underplayed her drive and the ball dropped into a stream lying between her and the green. . . . [She] decided to go after her ball which was floating down stream. Her husband, who was following her around the course, went along to help. They stepped into a rowboat and headed toward the ball as it lazily drifted [downstream]. . . . Leaning over the side of the rowboat, the persistent woman golfer slashed at the ball time and again with a niblick* [nine-iron], *while she and her husband kept count of the strokes. They were nearly a mile and a half away*

from the tee when she at last managed to connect cleanly with the ball and send it out of the water. . . . Nothing that might have happened would have daunted the woman at this stage of her battle with the elusive sphere. She tracked the ball down to its hiding place in the brush, pounded it out to a clearing and proceeded to play it back to the green. She reached the end of her journey eventually and triumphantly, holing out in exactly 166 strokes, the greatest number on record for a single hole.

While a single poor shot can evoke real agony, terrible scores need not always cause great pain. At some point a sequence of painfully bad shots turns from tragedy to hilarity. Several instances from the British Open found in *Golfer's Miscellany* make that clear. In the very first British Open at Prestwick in 1860, a competitor took a 21 on one hole. In the 1935 Open at Muirfield, a Scottish player started 7, 10, 5, 10, and took 65 shots to reach the ninth hole. He recorded another 10 at the eleventh and decided to retire at the twelfth, where he still lay in a bunker after having taken four shots without regaining the fairway. In the 1950 Open at Troon, a German amateur took a 15 on the short eighth, the famous Postage Stamp Hole. In a qualifying round in the 1965 British Open at Southport, a self-described American professional from Milwaukee shot 221 for 36 holes. He broke the record with a second round 113. At the tournament's conclusion, he admitted he was "a little discouraged and sad." He added that he had entered the tournament because he was "after the money."

Equally painful stories of golfers' undoings are a result of forces beyond the golfers themselves. Few stories rival the tale of the straw hat of J. C. Snead in the Tournament Players Championship at Sawgrass in Florida. On the fourth hole, a wind gusting to fifty miles an hour blew Snead's hat off his head and carried it forty yards up an embankment onto the green, where it ran into and moved his ball. Given a two-stroke penalty, Snead futilely protested, "I can't putt with my hat." Snead went on to three-putt the hole for good measure.

If this incident was ludicrous, equally incongruous and painfully hilarious was what happened to Leonard Thompson in the 1978 Quad Cities Open. A tee fell from his caddie's ear directly in the line of his rolling eagle putt, assuring Thompson's miss and a two-stroke penalty to boot.

A fellow caddie told me how another caddie cost his member four penalty strokes on the same hole. The caddie failed to pull out the pin in time and it was hit by his player's explosion shot. However, just as it was hit, out came the pin and the caddie stumbled backwards falling on another player's ball, costing his member another two strokes. The member was furious. He sent the caddie in and blamed him for the loss of the match, even though he was six strokes behind at the time the penalties were incurred. The player's pain won him only the mirth of others.

A Horizon of Pains

Golf's pains extend from mild irritation, frustration, and disappointment to despair and self-loathing. It is as difficult to put these pains under the same roof as it is to consider golf's pleasures as belonging to the same family. Pain, suffering, and despair are no more easily calculated than pleasure, happiness, and ecstasy.

Some players simply do not grasp the game and refuse to admit that they cannot perfectly command their mind and body. They reject the notion that winning implies many losses and refuse to admit the most obvious truth that Aristotle, the greatest of the philosophers, taught: There are infinitely more ways to miss the target than to hit it.

When the likelihood of error is joined to the golfer's quest for perfection, part of the mystery of why golf produces such an immense range of pain vanishes. "Golf," as Don Mahon said, "can be considered the practice of disappointment." It is hard to list all the ways in which golfers suffer disappointment. The golfer can experience the diverse unpleasant sensations that arise from the feel, sight, sound, and consequences of a poorly struck shot. Aside from misaiming or striking the ball weakly, the player can whiff the ball, top it, skull it, chunk it, slice it, sky it, hook it, or (the most horrible of blows) shank it. Or the player can even hit the ball twice with the same stroke, an error that caused then-unknown, aspiring Taiwanese player, T. C. Chen, to fail in his amazing final-day bid to win the 1985 U.S. Open at Oakland Hills.

Any misstruck blow can cut the golfer to the quick. In a single instant, a magic streak ends. Pain comes as either an overpowering sensation or a slow, sinking feeling, as when the player sees a well-struck shot gently yield to wind and slide out of bounds. A simple miscalculation or an unfortunate hop can bring a championship bid (or even a career) to an end.

Of Rage & Fury

Some of the sharpest pains can arise from an opponent's luck. Victory is lost to an opponent's errant ball taking a lucky bounce, caroming off another ball, hitting a member of the gallery and ending up on the green, or, finding its way back in bounds thanks to a fan's friendly foot mashie.

Indeed, an opponent's luck can inflict a crushing defeat. According to Peter Dobereiner, Lee Trevino's luck denied Tony Jacklin his fourth British Open at Muirfield in 1972. In some way, it also ended Jacklin's golf career. On the third day, Trevino holed an outrageous putt on the fourteenth; another on the fifteenth; sank a chip shot on the sixteenth; drained another long putt on the seventeenth; and sank a hard chip shot on the eighteenth. Trevino's closing five birdies produced a 66, which gave him a one stroke lead over Jacklin, who shot a solid 67. The fourth round, which again found them paired together, was more crippling for Jacklin.

They were level as they stood on the seventeenth tee. Trevino hit a poor drive and was duly punished when his ball found a pot bunker. Muirfield probably has the most penal fairway bunkers in the world and it was impossible for Trevino to advance the ball far from this cavernous hazard. Jacklin hit a perfect drive. Trevino chopped his ball out into the fairway and then hooked his third shot into the rough, still a long way short of the green. Jacklin's approach left him within chipping distance and sitting pretty for a birdie. Trevino, on the other hand, would have to work hard to save his par and that prospect vanished when his pitch from the rough went through the green and finished in a dreadful sandy lie.

Jacklin counselled himself not to try anything too fancy. Safety does it. As a result of this slightly defensive attitude he left his chip shot 15 feet short. He was still firmly in the driving seat, however, for Trevino's problem was acute. Trevino later admitted that at this point he mentally conceded the Open to Jacklin. He had enjoyed more than his ration of luck for one championship. However, he could not walk up and shake Jacklin's hand and call it a day. The shot had to be played, the formalities observed. He took his wedge and made what in his reconciled frame of mind was a perfunctory chop at the ball. Possibly it was precisely because he was not trying too hard on the shot and swinging with no trace of nervous tension that the contact was perfect. The ball skipped onto the green and rolled sweetly into the hole.

The blood drained from Jacklin's face. His heart sank into his boots. What other clichés are there to describe his feelings? Oh yes, his world collapsed. He swore inwardly and passionately. It had started again. Destiny was on Trevino's side. That is no kind of thought to entertain as you set yourself to the putt which can win you the Open. Jacklin missed, the ball sliding four feet past the hole. He felt physically sick and missed the return.

In the space of a few moments a hole which he had played in masterly fashion from tee to green had cost him a six while his rival had chopped about like a hacker and come up with a par five. It was too much for the human spirit to endure. . . .

Tony Jacklin is an ebullient creature and naturally resilient. After this crushing experience it took some time before he was his old gregarious self and rationalizing Muirfield as one of those things which happen in golf. Time heals most wounds but I believe that some part of Jacklin's psyche died on the seventeenth green on 15 July 1972, and that he was never quite the same golfer again.

Many golf stories are about broken clubs and broken hearts. My great aunt May, a World War One nurse, was not alone in the annals of amateur golf when she made her exit from the game by dumping her clubs into the canal into which her ball had just plopped. She did not, however, rival Ky Laffoon, whose place in Bruce Nash and Allan Zullo's *The Golf Hall of Shame* was secured by truly hangman-like antics. "Laffoon," they wrote,

*focused most of his anger on his clubs, which he brutalized
in ways more suited for the Spanish Inquisition. He
drowned putters, hanged drivers, and dragged irons
behind his car. . . . [At the Jacksonville Open] he trod
ankle deep into a creek, shoved the club under the water,
and screamed, "Drown you poor bastard, drown!"*

Nash and Zullo reported other instances of Laffoon's anger,
but none is as notorious as his road torture.

*"One time Ky just putted terribly," recalled Sam Snead.
"Ol' Ky was so mad at his putter that he tied it to the back
of his car and dragged it the whole way to the next
tournament, four hundred miles away. When I asked him
why he did it, he said that his putter deserved to be
humiliated because of the way it behaved. So it bounced
along back there for hundreds of miles, and when we
finally arrived, there was nothing left but a jagged shaft."
(Before his death, Laffoon disputed the story. "It was a
wedge," he said. "I was just trying to grind the edge.")*

Bernard Darwin, grandson of famous scientist Charles
Darwin and an accomplished Cambridge golfer, reacted to his
failed shots with notable fury. His tantrums, which may or
may not have been connected to "the origin of the species,"
were memorable. On one occasion, he fell to his knees, tore
clumps of turf from the ground with his teeth, and then
howled, "Oh God, now are you satisfied?"

The Fateful Shot

The player is often drawn to a type of bad shot. It clings to
him like fate itself. He can't play a given hole, course, or lost

round of a tournament without striking this fateful shot. No matter how well he is playing, the bad shot takes hold of him and he cannot free himself of it. He can't think of anything else. Anxiety encircles him. It captures his inner eye; he is its prisoner. Just before he hits the ball, the idea of the bad shot seizes him. It controls his body, distorts his muscles, and determines his swing. As if predestined, he looks up to see his ball follow the very path he foresaw. Or yet he sees the fruit of his resistance against it as his ball follows a nearly opposite path and he does not hit the hook (or slice) he feared, but creates a great push (pull) that sends his ball hurtling out-of-bounds.

An error, and the fear of it, can fate a player's game to destruction. Over several seasons, he plays his game in the shadow of the fateful shot. Over time he begins to think of himself as the bad tree from which bad fruit is born.

The more the player tries to overcome his error, the more pronounced it becomes and the more it takes him in its grip. His mind needs only to whisper it in advance of his shot and he hits the shot he fears. Or, no sooner does the player believe that he is beyond a given flaw, having beaten it out of himself by hours and hours on the practice range or by extensive competitive play, than it unexpectedly reappears. In time, the player—often a hooker who cannot learn to be a fader, or a slicer who can't hook—resigns himself to this error as if it were in his blood and the stars.

One player I knew dubbed himself "Duck Hook." Every time he hit an ugly, low, spinning hook, he shouted out his nickname. An old caddie friend of mine, who started golf with me at the country club's old hole, started golf with a burst. His intensity and intelligence convinced me that he was to be the best of us, until, thanks to an overpronated wrist, a case of the shanks overran his entire iron game. He shanked every iron he hit, long irons as well as short irons. Neither his determination, which was considerable, nor the advice of others, which was plentiful, made any difference. His plight of shanking shot after shot was put on display day after day and led him to quit the game altogether.

Even fine players do not escape fatal flaws. Like a mysterious disease, one day it shows up, and thereafter remains. Sometimes it is dormant, sometimes virulent; but it is always there, lurking, ready to surface when least expected. Golfing legend Tom Weiskopf, one of the great swingers in golf history, was recently interviewed on the last day of a PGA championship in which he played very well, but putted poorly. He diagnosed his own illness. He said his problem is that he no longer putts immediately after looking up toward the hole the second time. Pity Weiskopf! How terrible it must be! He plays knowing that once he has looked thrice, all is lost, for he should have only looked twice.

The Jumps, the Yips, & the Short-Putt Blues

Putting—this separate game within the game, in which the player rolls the ball a mere few feet after having struck it hundreds of yards—has cursed many of the game's greatest players. The great turn-of-the-century player, six-time British Open champion Harry Vardon (considered by many the equal of Jones), was one such player. He wrote in his book *The Progressive Golfer*, "I missed thousands of short putts in the past fifteen years, putts which count every bit as much as great long shots." Nobody, Vardon remarked, can say that putting demands skill, only confidence. Vardon's flaw, which he called "the jump," was what contemporary golfers call the "yips," a dreadful disease that, despite legions of proposed cures by contemporary physiologists, medical clinics, and amateur therapists, has brought many a fine golfer to the end of his game. (Vardon attributed the jump's cause to anxiety and an overly active right hand. It amounted, in his opinion, to an unwarranted tightening of the muscles.)

Nowhere, as Vardon knew, is pressure as great as it is on the green. For golfers it could be called "the table of pain." Here is where holes are ended and tournaments won and lost. The most wonderful shots, as Vardon knew so well, can be repealed by missing the shortest putts. Around the cup, where all players are equal, losses are irredeemable. When the "jumps" were upon Vardon, he faced holy terror. He said that two-foot putts frightened him most of all and that as he settled down to putt, the hole seemed to get increasingly smaller. "I am overcome," he said, "with the idea that in a moment it will vanish altogether." He confessed to missing putts as short as six inches. Sometimes he was so desperate for a cure that he resorted to putting with only his left hand. At other times he would rush to putt before the jumps took hold of him. He sought to "miss 'em quick." Vardon attributed his unprecedented sixth victory in the Open at Prestwick in 1914 to hiding his malady from his arch-rival and five-time Open champion, J. H. Taylor. Vardon believed that Taylor's confidence would have been immensely improved if Taylor had known Vardon was again suffering the jumps.

The great shot-maker and recovery-artist, Walter Hagen, ended his career in the 1930s when the yips took hold of him. Hagen is numbered among those who lost their mastery of the game when their putting left. For the past decade, Tom Watson, one of the game's greatest players, a winner of five British Opens, and formerly an excellent putter, has worn the shroud of missing short putts. Everyone knows—television shows it to the whole world—that if Watson could sink three- and four-foot putts, he would still be one of the game's truly dominant players. The magic of his great swing has been cut off at the very threshold of the cup. He who once played in the heavens has been forced to suffer the vagaries of this lesser earthly kingdom.

Greater Pains & Corruptions

Beyond defeating the will and breaking the heart of a player, golf can corrupt him. Any serious player knows the main text of an unwritten book titled "The Temptations of Golf." Clubhouses are havens for those players whom the game has not only defeated, but corrupted with alcohol and gambling.

Bernard Darwin described a rare form of corruption. In *Second Shots*, he noted that those who have all the golf they want are similar to the kid who, turned loose in the chocolate factory, loses all taste for chocolate. Darwin described a golfer who grew "to be such an epicure about that game that, if he ever plays at all, it is only to essay a particularly subtle spoon shot at a particular hole when a particular wind is blowing, and that in solitude." This epicure of a golfer ended up not playing at all. He only walked, observed, and carried a club, about which Darwin commented: "For all the 'music' in the shaft and the fine lines of the head, it is no more than a mere brute walking stick."

Golf tempts a superficial breed of players to confuse the game with life. Admittedly, it is indeed hard to know life well without at times wishing to substitute a game for it. No average tempter, golf lures all its players with endless distraction from life itself. As French thinker, Blaise Pascal, observed: "Men and women prefer distraction to awareness." Golf offers endless opportunities for distraction with its many courses, endless tournaments, new techniques and equipment.

Anyone who knows golf well knows players who have lost their youth, careers, families, and fortunes to the game. While I have never heard of a priest who left the priesthood for the game, golf's literature is filled with stories of clergy who far preferred the game to their parishioners and theology. One parish priest always cut his Saturday confessions short so he could eat and make his twilight golf round, a ritual his parishioners knew well. He claimed his few poor shots made him tolerant of his parishioners' great and varied sins. Certainly the open and varied sensations of the course are invigoratingly straightforward when measured against the endless sinuosity of the human heart, and the tedium of human vice.

A devotee of the game who was not short of wit saw golf, rather than religion, as a way to a better world:

> *While theologies tend to disrupt, antagonize, and embitter humanity, games genialize the soul of man, and tend to peace, concord and loving kindness. . . . How much better the globe, if Buddha had had a motor-bicycle, Mohammed had been an international tennis player, and if Athanasius and Arius had been inseparable on a golf links.*

Golf, no doubt, serves as a substitute religion for some of its players. Golf mystics can pour their quests for ecstasy into obsessive searches for perfection. The complexity of the swing and the diversity of shots the game requires are standing invitations to escape the impurities of this world. Surely, golf's Byzantine rituals and rules are worthy of a heresy or two.

Of course, it should never be forgotten that for man golf is a labyrinth. The player can lose himself in the game. And what despair for the player who discovers that he lost himself to a game. As much as we wish it to be otherwise, even this royal and ancient game of golf cannot be a substitute for life.

*"A round of golf is really a struggle against
a terrifying horde of weaknesses."*
— Leslie Schon, **A Tribute to Golf**

*"[The Golfer] wages a warfare against self. . . . It is not a
wrestle with Bogey; it is not a struggle with your mortal foe;
it is physiological, and moral fight with yourself;
it is a test of mastery over self."*
— Arnold Haultain, **The Mystery of Golf**

8

Character

WHEN AS A YOUTH I heard someone say that "golf was a
game about character," I surely didn't think about how character depends upon integrity, or about how integrity requires
honesty. I never once considered the nature and source of the
intelligence that honesty requires, or considered why this intelligence, bountiful in some, is so absent in others. After all,
this was all beyond me, as I was only a boy.

When I heard about golf and character, I thought immediately about how golfers cheated. I knew there was no poor lie
which a golfer, on occasion, wouldn't be tempted to improve,
no bad shot he might not wish to hit again, and no golfing
rule he could not find a reason to revise. I already knew and

practiced most of Henry Beard's "official exceptions to the rules of golf." That is, I knew the justification for taking a shot over because of "the audible interference with the swing," be it a whisper, zipper, fart, or snicker. I revoked dozens of shots because I wasn't "really trying" or the results of the shot were "manifestly" or "intrinsically" unfair. Finally, I affirmed the right to choose the best of two or three shots.

Some of the members I caddied for were blatant cheaters. They counted inaccurately; improved lies; declared the need for winter rules when summer rules were posted; conceded themselves putts they didn't deserve; took mulligans; and did a variety of other things to post better scores than they had earned. They frequently yielded to the temptation to hit short putts over again. And I knew my own sins better than theirs. I even remember how, on the ninth and final hole of my first high school tournament, I set my bag on the branch of a bush to remove it from the path of my nine-iron shot to the green. I may have saved myself a stroke, but not the long, painful memory of such a flagrant violation of the rules of golf.

With a confessionally-trained Catholic conscience in place, I was aware of golf's temptations. I was conscious of the way self-deception played an even more insidious part in my game than lying and cheating. I knew how I always invented reasons why I should have played better. At the head of the list of excuses were the condition of the course, the weather, and disturbances by others.

I would start out a round intending to keep score as if I were playing in a tournament. However, often only within a hole or two and after a few bad shots, I would start taking and counting second shots. I would end the round with a score for my best ball. Or, at other times, midway through a round in which my score soared way beyond acceptable limits, I would declare it a practice round. I remember once in a caddie tournament trying to convince myself that the round didn't really count. (My friend, Don Olsen, had a friend who never shot the front nine over par because he never played past the sixth hole, which returned to the clubhouse, when he was over par.)

Like other golfers, I replayed rounds with my "mouth mashie," insisting even when I was playing well that "I could have shot better if only. . . ." I found medal play more difficult than match play. It was a rigorous discipline to keep accurate score. I preferred match play, which at the time was the format of our caddie championships and high school matches. I found it easier to leave each hole behind and start anew. It didn't matter if I got a five, seven, or an "X," as I had either won or lost the hole. I also liked the notion that the match itself justified hitting risky shots forbidden in medal play. If the shot failed, I was absolved from blame as it was hit for the sake of the match. Perhaps the greatest bonus in match play was that short putts were often conceded. Indeed, the game sets too high a standard for its players. "There is more likelihood that a golfer will be more honest about his taxes than his game," was an aphorism commonly recited at the club.

Is it not worth asking why golfers play a game that so challenges their honesty and in which self-delusion is a common condition? No doubt, one reason why a person plays golf is a fascination with the self-revelation that the game yields.

It is stunning to see a player go into a total rage. I once saw this in the Fall of my second year of caddying at the country club. The player, who usually wore colorful pants, had never before made any unusual displays of temper when I caddied for him. The sums he was playing for that day were typically small—a dollar on the front, a dollar on the back, and a dollar for the eighteen. His opponent was a common opponent to whom he won and lost on a regular basis. The only difference that day was that he had reached, thanks to a slight tail wind and a fine three-wood shot, the front apron of the eighteenth green in two for the first time in his life.

A four would have easily won him the back nine and the eighteen, and a coveted par on the always difficult eighteenth. With the other three players and their caddies for an audience, he spent a lot of time lining up his shot, and asked that the pin be taken out. Then he took his faithful wood-handled chipper back and halfway down he quit altogether. The ball traveled less than fifteen of the required sixty feet to the hole and curved into the trap on the left. At first he stood and said nothing, and looked like he was going to cry. Then, without warning, he took his chipper in his hands, snapped it in two over his knee, and shouted "Mother f—." Repeating the phrase twice, he sailed the two parts of the chipper up toward the large verandah of the clubhouse where twenty or thirty formally-attired women were gathered. He then took his large leather bag from me and threw it down on the ground, hollering "Mother f—" several times. He jumped up and down on the bag before he started hurling balls from it. With each ball he threw, he hollered "Mother f—," then picked up his bag and threw it into the deep sand trap that contained his ball, bellowing out "Mother f—" one more time before he stomped down the hill and up toward the clubhouse.

Players and caddies alike were at first stunned into silence, until one caddie began to snicker when another whispered "Mother f—" just loud enough so all heard him. The uncomprehending women on the verandah peered down at three men and four boys laughing uncontrollably.

Pressure

When I heard the phrase "Golf reveals character," I also thought, as did my peers, about how well the player withstood pressure. Golf for me, and for all avid young golfers, was about pressure. It was about competition and hitting necessary shots. Pressure, I already knew, could take a variety of forms. It could wake a player up, put an edge on his game, cause sweating, dizziness, anxiety, constriction or (as professionals report) a crushing tightness in the chest, threatening a player's ability to breathe regularly.

A member of our high school team always had to urinate during the first few holes of a match. This caused little trouble at Chandler Park, our home course, whose holes were lined by bushes. However, in our junior year, the city finals were played on a wide open course. There wasn't a tree or bush in sight and there were spectators all over the course. He took two double bogies on the first two holes, and still he had not found a place to relieve himself. Finally, he turned his back to us and urinated directly into his bag, which he extended straight in front of him. He went down the third fairway with urine dripping out of his bag and for the remainder of the nine, he wiped the handle of his club before each shot. We all played poorly but laughed a lot.

Any observer of golf knows that there are players who simply cannot play well in competition. There are even players who don't play well in the company of others. Just the idea that someone is watching their swing makes them tense.

Every golfer experiences some pressure every time he steps on a course. The first shot of a round—particularly in a tournament or on a great course like Prestwick or St. Andrews—carries with it all the anxiety that goes with the beginning of any great undertaking. The golfer on the first tee can worry about a lot of things, as he can even wonder (as silly as it is) whether he has forgotten how to play or whether he will whiff the ball. He can't help but believe, even though he knows better, that his first shot will indicate how the rest of his round will go. The great Walter Hagen himself went to the first tee hoping simply to hit the ball solidly.

Players experience different types of pressure throughout a round, ranging from a gentle tensing of muscles to outright panic. Pressure's origins are found in the simple act of attentiveness and taking the outcome of something seriously. It can concentrate around a given shot, a type of shot, a single hole, a run of holes, a round, or a tournament. It can intensify across rounds and across entire seasons of a player's career.

Pressure is not always harmful, as it often elevates the golfer's play. In fact, some players associate golf's pleasures with its pressure. Like the gambler or other thrill-seeker, a golfer can be addicted to the stimulation generated by tension and suspense. Pressure as a stimulant makes the player feel alive. Jim Bishop wrote of the good player's need for pressure:

> *The hacker dreams of relaxing, as though in golf, lassitude will cut ten strokes from his game. **Au contraire**. He who relaxes is ruptured. Good players find that a mixture of equal parts of tension, hatred, and self-loathing insure a good round. It is not only permissible, but desirable to despise the course, the ball, wives, children, and weather and the score.*

The greatness of certain professionals was spawned by pressure, Hogan being a favorite example. "Hogan," Mark McCormak wrote, "appeared to have the indefinable quality of bringing himself to his supreme peak when his need was most urgent and the pressure greatest." And of his winning performance in the 1953 British Open at Carnoustie, where he improved with each round—73, 71, 70, and 68—McCormak cited Bernard Darwin, who said of Hogan's final round, "One was quite certain Hogan could have played a 64, for he gave you the distinct impression that he was capable of getting whatever score he needed to win."

As much as professionals need pressure to perform their best, pressure in a tournament can reach staggering proportions, making seasoned professionals tremble. Players describe how at times in tournaments they felt out of control. Their hands, body, and mind seemed beyond their command. It became a feat for them to keep a drive on the widest fairway, to get a hundred-yard wedge onto the green, or to hole a two-foot putt.

Players usually find it easier to come from behind than to bear the pressure of leading a tournament over several rounds. An oppressive sense of dread can settle down on the leader of a tournament. This is confirmed by Greg Norman's collapse at the 1996 Masters, when he held a commanding lead for three rounds, yet self-destructed and lost by a big margin to Nick Faldo on the final day. Once a player begins to feel he will lose, he is in trouble. He lacks words to counsel himself. He remembers tournaments he lost and he even postulates the existence of a superior force that doesn't want him to win.

A single good shot, or a lucky break, like holing a sculled wedge or benefiting from a favorable bounce off a sprinkler head, could break the oppressive sense that has settled down on him. Another player or caddie might help restore the player's lucidity. A master caddie from the American tour, Pete Bender, is reported in a recent issue of *Golf* (May, 1994), to have saved an earlier tournament for Greg Norman. Holding a three-stroke lead on that last day of the 1986 British Open, Norman snap-hooked his drive off the sixth tee. Bender grabbed Norman by the shirt and said to him: "Look, Greg, you're playing too quick, and you've got to slow down. You're the best player in the field. You're going to win this tournament if you take your time and enjoy it and don't press the issue." Norman slowed his pace and won the tournament by five strokes.

As painful as pressure is, what would the game be without it? Questions of who will break—and when, how, and why—all add to the game's excitement. Surely there is pleasure in the suspense of waiting for a player to come undone and the accompanying delight of seeing how he does come undone. As boys, still half-believing in our exemption from the weakness of humanity, we took a particularly pitiless delight in seeing golfers succumb to pressure—or to use one of our many expressions, "blow up," "come apart," "crack," "fold," "come unraveled," "cave in," "not take it," or the most favorite phrase of all, "choke." Our boyish fascination with the cracking up of others was as old as Greek tragedy itself.

As if he is watching a drama, an observer of golf experiences a mixture of anxiety and anguish as he follows a tight round of golf. The match's conclusion can bring a sense of nobility when its outcome is resolved by skill and strength of character. It can produce a feeling of pathos, or even farce, when a player is not at all equal to the test, or his loss is a result of sheer accident. The observer's higher side is delighted by seeing a fellow person withstand a test, while his darker side enjoys watching another (not so different from himself!) come undone in the face of stiff competition or unexpected misfortune.

As Shakespeare's tragedies offer us the collapses of kings, so golf on television invites millions to view high drama and mighty failures. I asked for examples of failures under pressure from an avid golfing friend, and he recalled instantly: Doug Sanders missed a four-foot putt on the eighteenth at St. Andrews allowing Nicklaus to tie him for the British Open, which Nicklaus won in the playoff the next day. He recalls Ballesteros duck-hooking a five-iron shot into the pond on the fifteenth at Augusta, ending his run at Nicklaus and a chance for victory in the Masters. And, he can't forget how, with an audience of millions, Johnny Miller shanked a seven iron on the sixteenth at Pebble Beach in the last round of the U.S. Open, a shot Miller still claims wasn't a shank.

More pathetic than these failures, yet as testing of character, are tournaments lost to rule infractions. In the course of a match, Watson once advised Trevino to play the ball in his stance. Trevino thanked Watson for his advice and a television fan telephoned the officials, who added two strokes to Watson's score. Equally astute television fans cost Craig Stadler $37,000 and disqualification from the 1987 Andy Williams Open when they informed officials that by placing a towel under his knees to avoid kneeling in the mud, he had violated Rule 13-3: He had improved his stance and not taken the required two-stroke penalty.

Unsigned, missigned, and faultily-calculated score cards have sometimes stolen tournaments and broken hearts before a watching nation, as when a Hawaiian-born housewife lost the 1957 U.S. Women's Open for signing a scorecard on which her playing companion had mistakenly entered a five for a six. Doug Sanders lost the 1966 Pensacola for accidentally failing to sign his card; an official whispered the disqualification into Sanders's ear as he held court in the press room.

Some infractions and fines can only be considered sheer farces. As reported in *The Golf Hall of Shame*, Tommy Bolt made a "shot heard around the world." In the 1959 Memphis Invitational Open at the Colonial Country Club, Bolt was fined for intentionally farting just before his opponent putted. Offended spectators reported Bolt's deed to official Bob Rosburg, who fined Bolt, the 1958 U.S. Open Champion, "for conduct unbecoming a professional golfer." Bolt protested his fine—which at the time was a stiff $250—bellowing "Damn

it! You guys are trying to take all the color out of the game!"
When asked later about this incident, Bolt replied, "That
story got blown out of proportion."

Certainly the weapons of a coarser and more competitive
era of golf have been steadily declared out of bounds since the
1950s, the decade when bodies, kitchens, and bathrooms became sanitized.

Needling

Allan Robertson alluded to another dark (and now largely re-
pressed) side of golf when he ironically noted: "It appeals to
the higher feelings of humanity to see your rival in a bunker."
The best golfer at the public course where I played, a professional fireman dubbed "Fireman Al," played golf as well as
any public links player in the city. One day Fireman Al told
us boys the secret of winning through needling. "It doesn't
really matter how you needle another player. It only matters
that he believes you are needling him, for this both gets him
angry at you for doing it and at himself for being bothered by
it. Once he is caught between these two bothersome thoughts,
his anger grows and he will find it harder and harder to play
his normal game." Having said that, he gave us particular advice about types of needling: "Never give a bad putter a
putt—no matter its length. Sooner or later, he will miss one
and then he will have to deal with himself. Talk a lot to quiet
players. When really desperate, accuse your opponent of
cheating—miscounting, teeing up his ball in the rough, it
doesn't matter—just imply you think he might be cheating."
We were later bemused to hear that Fireman Al got punched
in the nose for accusing Policeman John of cheating.

Our world is increasingly sanitized of nicknames and is essentially devoid of open rivalries. Accordingly, pleasure derived from defeating a fellow player is not as readily admitted.

Contemporary golf sensibility has less room in it for games-manship. Medal play, rather than match play, prevails; therefore, it is not polite to take pleasure in an opponent's bad shots and misfortunes. Gloating is considered to be a moral defect. It is, moreover, considered poor sporting conduct to cause another player to hit a bad shot.

Golf today is far removed from the time when match play commanded, and when players like Walter Hagen (the tricky Ulysses of modern golf) used all sorts of artifices to confuse and unsettle opponents. He particularly liked to convince opponents that he used one club, when, in fact, he used another. He also frequently pretended to arrive on the first tee after having stayed out all night. This gave him an air of nonchalance, indifference and invulnerability. In a playoff for the U.S. Open in 1919, on a morning after Hagen actually had stayed out all night, he asked his opponent, Mike Brady, on the second tee, " 'Listen, Mike, hadn't you better roll down those sleeves?' 'What for?' 'The gallery can see your muscles twitching.' Brady then walloped a murderous hook that cost him two strokes on the hole." Hagen won the Open by one stroke, after using a rule to identify his ball on the eighteenth as a way to drop and clean his ball from a buried lie.

In that era golf was about knowing and beating your man. Knowing how to exploit weaknesses in your opponent's character—vanity, gullibility, or especially anger—was a matter of pride. Until the 1950s, ruses of all sorts (such as saying one thing to one's caddie while doing another, or purposely hitting a long club a short distance, or reminding one's opponent of his known weaknesses), were commonly accepted roads to victory. A classic test of insults and threats occurred in the 1946 Western Amateur between upper-class Frank Stranahan and working-class Smiley Quick, who had even worked in a circus. Their rivalry, "a test of character," is described in *The Golf Hall of Shame*:

*Smiley began giving Frank the "treatment," figuring that
his pampered rival wouldn't know how to meet the
challenge. At first it was hard-edged ribbing as Quick
entertained the spectators with dire predictions of
Stranahan's fate: "Watch him hit it right into the bunker,"
or, "He couldn't make that putt if he dug a trench to the
hole."*

*But Frank dished it right back: "He talks when he's
scared," and, "The only thing he knows how to swing is a
trapeze."*

*Soon words weren't enough. On the green, they rudely
stood in the lines of each other's putts, moved about just
as the other was putting, or jingled change in their pockets.
Once, Stranahan putted out and arrogantly strolled on to
the next tee, leaving Smiley to putt out alone. Whenever
Frank hit into the rough, Quick followed him and watched
as if he suspected Stranahan would try to improve his lie.
This rancor and vitriol lasted throughout the entire 36-
hole match and into a sudden-death playoff.*

*"All your millions won't help you now," Smiley growled
at Frank as they teed off on the 37th hole. "I'm going to
put the spurs to you now."*

"With what?" snapped Stranahan.

*"It won't take much with that sissy swing you've got,"
retorted Smiley.*

*At the 39th hole, Quick's antagonism turned even more
hostile when he threatened Stranahan by saying, "I'm
going to end this match now. Then I'm going to take care
of you out behind the clubhouse."*

*Frank didn't say a word. He let his putter answer by
sinking a 12-footer for a birdie to win the overtime match.
Smiley . . . walked over, halfheartedly shook Frank's hand
and disappeared.*

There is nothing left which even whispers the likes of the Quick-Stranahan match. Contemporary players resemble more the carefully manicured courses on which they play. Contemporary players are more polite, considerate, and caring, even if they have not yet entirely degenerated into that breed of players Robert Hunter feared would emerge.

> *There may yet come among us effeminate souls who would have all the fairways of asphalt, boarded high on both sides so that all shots will be equally good, whether topped, skyed, pulled, or sliced. In the last days of our degeneracy it may be urged that all fairways be down-grade, with well formed grooves to the hole, so that every man, woman, and child will invariably hole out in one.*

Fortunately, the triumph of tameness and politeness is not complete. As is evidenced by the intensity of serious contemporary matches, there still remains a pleasure, not only in testing one's own, but in testing the character of another. An important pleasure of golf is still associated with attempting to discover if one really has "the right stuff." Refined manners have not yet dissolved the desire for triumph over others. A winning character on the course has not yet been identified with being a swell fellow, even though golf's broadcasters would lead us to believe that professionals are philanthropists who play for charities and are winners because they are nice.

Golf's attractions are not merely associated with competition with courses and opponents, but they are tied to the wars within the player. As paradoxical as it is, there is truth to the notion that we love the game for the pains it causes us. Hunter had part of the truth when he wrote,

> *It is not the love which has drawn men like a magnet for hundreds of years to this royal and ancient pastime; on the*

contrary, it is the maddening difficulty of it. One speaks of masters, but who has mastered even its simplest details? "It's a cruel sport," said its greatest master Vardon, when he missed that famous putt, which he or any child could have kicked in. But that is what fascinates. . . . What is more engaging than to see how golf infuriates some big brute. . . . What is so delectable as to see him in nervous tremor as he stands on the tee, glaring fiercely at that still, white, little ball! How the game torments the adventurous soul! . . . Golf beats us all, and that is the chief reason we shall never cease loving her, nor ever give up our attempt to subdue her.

In his *If You Play Golf, You're My Friend,* Harvey Penick gives an excellent example of how an early defeat can be a blessed defeat. He tells how at the Southwest Conference Tournament at the Colonial Country Club in Texas (known as Hogan's Alley), a young aspiring player, Dan Jenkins, was defeated. With Hogan himself in the gallery, Jenkins, who was even with his rival, recovered on a par-four sixteenth hole from an adjacent fairway with a wonderful iron shot that left him six inches from the cup, only to have his opponent hole his shot. Broken, he three-putted the next hole to be defeated two-and-one. The following year, the same young man in the Southwest Conference medal tournament three-putted sixteen times in 72 holes to finish third. Instead of pursuing a career in golf, Jenkins went on to become a well-known sportswriter and novelist. Penick claims he has always wanted to say to Jenkins: "Well, Dan, think how lucky you are. If Morris hadn't holed out that seven-iron, and if you had three-putted only twelve times . . . you might today be an assistant pro at Goat Hills."

The wisdom embodied in Penick's story is that you can win when you lose and lose when you win. Initial success can cast young people's lives in small molds from which they may never break. And the pleasures of golf are small when measured against other possible pleasures of life. As a young man, Penick himself was blessed with an experience. On the practice range one day, he saw Sam Snead rifle ball after ball. Penick wisely concluded on the spot that the pro tour was not for him.

Now that I am older, I understand the various ways that golf tests character. For the serious players, it tests their courage, patience, prudence, tenacity, judgment and, finally, their wisdom itself. I remember how one of our club's assistant pros, especially disgusted because he had lost a match to one of the members, blurted out as he put his glove and balls in his bag, "This damn game takes your money, your soul, and your life." I was too young then to grasp all that resonated in his statement. I now know that a golfer can substitute the game for a life. Justified as a momentary flight from the day's affairs, golf is unjustified as an escape from life. Caught in the labyrinth of perfecting their games, golfers have sacrificed family, children, and everything else to it.

Walter Hagen's wife divorced him for his obsession with the game. A 1937 newspaper article reported, "Mrs. Walter Hagen, America's golf widow No. 1, signaled the opening of the golf season today by advising all women against marrying confirmed golfers." Having just won a divorce from Hagen, she forecast that marriages with ardent golfers are destined to end on the rocks, saying "Walter lived golf, asleep and awake." He practiced his swing before and after supper. He obviously did not court her nightly affection, for "He would pause in his shorts, while preparing to retire, to take a couple of swings before turning out the lights." If that wasn't enough to bury a wedge in their married life, the very mention of the word "golf" wrecked their dinner parties. Before guests had finished eating, they would engage in practicing their grips on silverware. "For me," Mrs. Hagen reported, "the evening would be ruined."

Other players lost more than dinner parties and wives to the game. A 1938 newspaper article reports that while America was caught in the grips of the Great Depression, former great national amateur champion Jerry Travis was caught in the depths of his own depression. At the age of forty-nine, he was broke, jobless, homeless, and had a family to support. With no means of income, Travis was driven to participate in a national benefit auction for him, raffling off his only remaining golf club. The rusted mashie he was auctioning off was his magic wand. It was the first club he bought when he was fourteen. He used it to win four national amateurs and one national open. The sale severed his last physical tie to the game. Travis confessed,

> *I hate to use anything connected with the sport to make money, but there is a limit to a man's pride when his wife and children need food and shelter. I have done everything I could for the past six years to make my own way, but I haven't been able to make my own way. So if the USGA wants my club, I'll sell it.*

Travis was only one champion who proved that golf's glories do not secure a golfer against life's vicissitudes. Golf does not build the character, supply the wisdom, or provide the wealth required by a long and good life.

"The two best schools for mind and manners, says the sage, are the Court and the Camp. He might have added a third. He who would attain self-knowledge should frequent the links. If one seriously essays the task, one will 'find oneself.'"
—Arnold Haultain, **The Mystery of Golf**

9

Wisdom

THERE IS MUCH I DISBELIEVE about golf's beneficence, and as much as I admire Arnold Haultain's *The Mystery of Golf*, I don't agree with his assertion that, "It takes a strong character to play strong golf," unless he conceded—which he did not—that "the strong character" could be composed of a lot of vices. Or, unless he was willing to grant, which he did not, that too much attention to golf might contribute to the narrow focus of imagination, intellect, and morality of his "player of strong character." Golf might lead the player, already predisposed in this direction, to restrict his empathy, reason, and imagination to a game at the expense of more important things in life. Indeed, off the course the dedicated golfer might prove to be but another boring specialist. And I can conceive of no single prevalent culture around the game, the clubhouse, or the profession that assures players intellectual or moral integrity. Nor do I share Haultain's notion that "he who would attain self-knowledge should frequent the links."

For similar reasons, I also don't agree with Jerry Travis when he sees golf as a way to know the world and the self. I don't believe he was accurate when he asserted, "Breadth of character is readily measured under the microscope of golf's influence." And I think he got it wrong when he wrote:

> In our rounds of the links we encounter nearly all the little odds and ends of human emotions. We have codified the principles which tend to make our time on earth brighter and more fruitful—hard work, self-restraint, patience, courage, determination, perseverance and the three graces, faith, hope, and charity. They are the same in golf.

Obviously, Travis saw golf serving as the education of an upper-class Victorian good that preached the ideal person to be a unity of virtues of character and Christian graces.

Nevertheless, I do believe that the players who stay with golf over a long period do gain a kind of wisdom. By dedication over a long period to a craft, older golfers understand the reward of practice. By knowing a skill like golf, they realize that mind and body are not docile servants of even the keenest discipline. By a long acquaintance with the self, they admit that they have a temperament which character might control, but does not, or should not, command. By competing, they realize the game is a mixture of character and skill, while recognizing one's best does not assure victory. Furthermore, older players become aware of the combination of work and skill, grace and luck that shapes the careers of the small number of really great players. And, finally, they are aware that golf is not one, the self is not one, and there is no one way to play the game or live a life.

Humility is one virtue an older golfer is likely to have gained, for golf humbles in many ways. First, as Haultain pointed out, it is the still and interrogating ball of golf, not the moving and excusing ball of other sports, which repeatedly humbles the golfer. It is there by itself, waiting for us to command it. Yet it lies at the bottom of a long line of embarrassing, shameful, humiliating, and even guilt-inducing insubordinations that are perilous to every swing. The still ball proves that our minds don't always follow our wills and our bodies disobey our minds. And so we discover our swings are disobedient.

My friend Don Olsen draws more pessimistic lessons from the game. He wrote me:

> *When you wrote that "golfers . . . gain a kind of wisdom,"
> I would add the wisdom comes from an intense awareness
> of one's own ineptness, stupidity and ignorance. For
> instance, we keep trying to do that which we know we
> can't do. We are all madmen in need of reality therapy. I
> think of a scene in Faulkner's first novel when one
> character says, "It's a rotten old world and dying ain't half
> of it."*

Don continued:

> *We go out to the first tee, year after year, knowing we will
> fail and that the perfection we seek is but a fantasy, a
> foolish dream. Is the glory in the process, in the practice?
> Are we all Sisyphus with a club in our hands instead of a
> monumental boulder at our shoulder? . . . The hills we
> climb are named Oakmont, and Pebble Beach, and St.
> Andrews, and Goat Hills. We keep playing but we get
> nowhere.*

Second, every serious player of the game learns about flaws in his attitude towards himself and the game. He has, so to speak, ripped up the plankings of his inner house several times to reestablish a proper relation to the game. Like the ancient, meditative monk, he has embarked on several roads to learn golf's way. And only the most arrogantly narrow, or simply the least imaginative golfer does not glimpse how many vices and weaknesses exist in him both on and off the course.

Third, golf forces every player to look at his integrity. Does he work hard? Does he keep score honestly? Is the favorite club in his bag the alibi? Can he handle the rub of the green? How many different ways does he have to tell himself he doesn't really care but if he did he would have done better? Can he stay loyal to himself and the game on both good and bad days? From such questions as these no player emerges morally unscathed.

Fourth, by the measure of perfection (a mirror before which the old golfer wisely stands less and less), experienced golfers realize they are blessed if they can play at all and additionally blessed if they play well. They understand, though not necessarily with a statistician's exactitude, the application to their game of the religious truth that many are called and few are chosen. And they grasp that even the few who are elected in golf have bad rounds, seasons, and careers, and they are not immune from squandering their talents along with their lives on a game.

There is another important element composing the wisdom of the old golfers, as they are willing to mix the pleasures of the game and take them as they come. They do not seek the exclusive pleasure of victory. They do not insist on the ecstasies of golf's highest moments. By accepting and mixing diverse pleasures, they make the game richer, even if less passionate than for aspiring younger players. For wiser, older players, golf passes from romance to friendship.

They even come to treat the courses they play and the clubs they swing as part of their friendship with the game. They acquaint themselves with the character and history of the courses they play. They learn grasses. They appreciate changing conditions, and the testing winds that, as Bernard Darwin pointed out years ago, have yet to be given specific golfing names. (What should golfers call all the types of winds, from all the different directions, that so enhance their game?)

The older players find companionship on the course, and it invigorates them in mind and body. Unless their bodies fail them, older player can still compete—and compete proficiently, as the senior tour shows—into their sixties. They still experience the sensuous pleasures of sending a ball through space, driving one shot with a strong downwind, or kiting another with a high fade with a gusting crosswind. They can cause one putt to roll softly off the toe of the putter in order to slow its speed down the steep slope between the ball and the hole, or hook another putt with a touch of overspin to send it up across the long apron towards the distant hole. Even in their seventies, accomplished players can still hit wonderful shots, shots that fly as purely as they were conceived. And they can have the great pleasure of shooting a score equal to or less than their own age, like a current member at the Royal Liverpool who has already shot his age forty or so times.

A recent newspaper article in the *Minneapolis Star Tribune* tells of an old local player who believed he played his best golf in his sixties when he shot in the low eighties. The article notes that now, at 95, "He doesn't dally over his shots. He talks, he swings, the ball soars. He grabs his cart and walks again." He is quoted as saying, "The game is frustrating at any

age. But it's not complicated. You hit the ball, walk, and hit it
again. Even when the game's bad, the fresh air's great, the
birds are fascinating, and the conversation's worthwhile. . . .
As long as I can walk, I'll play."

Reflection adds to the pleasures of older players. They have
learned to play courses in their minds. They can remember
great rounds and players. While they need not be collectors of
clubs, balls, or other golf memorabilia, or readers of the history of the game—which provides great pleasure to its students—they can enjoy recollections of the game. The old,
who have a taste for it, can even take the clubs of their youth
(woodshafters and the early steel shafts that followed) and
test them on more primitive courses, where lie and roll have
to be calculated and the draw hook was required for distance
and to play in the wind. For the older golfer with money, a
golfing trip back to England, Scotland, or Ireland to play seaside courses can be a special delight, almost a pilgrimage.
There, where roughs and winds test their play, they can make
contact with the game's modern beginnings and play a more
hardy game. These courses are not manicured and carved by
cart paths, nor were they engineered to be picturesque or to
serve a target-like sport. The golf played then involved a wonderful elemental sense of hurling and clubbing balls through
space. There was a great need for raw cunning in shotmaking,
and players needed tenacity to fight back against strings of
bogies and double bogies when they were the common lot of
all who wandered into roughs worthy of their name.

Old players enjoy a more secure band of pleasures, while
the younger players are moved by more volatile feelings. For
the old, golf's pleasures are less ecstatic, but richer, gentler,
and more secure than they are for the young. Age, at least
when accompanied by wisdom, brings a recognition of limits
that, if not transformed into despair, frees older players from
the youthful and agonizing quest for the glory of perfection.

Wisdom allows the old player to place golf in perspective. He realizes that its pressures are self-imposed and that nothing of great consequence rides on the outcome of his play. The wise older player shapes the game to his own pleasures in a way that younger players, driven by idols of fame, cannot. He makes the game more comfortable. He can keep score and compete when he wishes. If he wishes to remain competitive, he can choose one of a variety of ways to compete. He can, if he chooses, even find alternative ways to count. He can play alone.

The solitary golfer can be the most privileged of golfers. He walks at his own gait. He plays at his own pace. He is at home on more primitive courses. He is even gleeful when the wind howls and the weather turns bad, emptying the course of its crowds of sunshine players. The solitary golfer plays in early Spring and late Fall, and, in some areas, even through the Winter. He has the pleasure of choosing his competition. He can compete with himself by trying to beat his previous best scores or shoot below his handicap. He can play a two-ball tournament against himself, playing one ball off the back professional tees, and the other off the men's tees. Or, he can imagine himself in a tournament of deadly seriousness, in which no lie is improved and no single putt conceded. Or, like the fisherman trolling for the single great muskie, he can play along, interested only in the occasional great shot or wonderful sequence of shots he can pull off. And if the course is empty, he can invent his own course, changing teeing areas and greens to invent more challenging holes. The solitary golfer need only stop momentarily to hit his shot. Nothing prevents the solitary golfer as he plays from exercising, meditating, praying, preparing a lecture, concluding a business deal, outlining a chapter of a book, or simply waiting to see what will pop into his mind. For him the pleasures of the course include the joys of the mind.

The wise player must know his own strengths and weaknesses, for without this wisdom the player commonly misjudges his own experience. He tends to over- or underestimate his own ability, mistake the quality of shots, or ignore the place of skill and luck in the game. Unavoidably, such a player regularly ends up by being mistaken even about his own pleasures and pains. He takes pleasure from what he does easily or by luck, while being pained by shots and scores that, given his game, should make him happy. Like the man who wanders through life with no understanding of himself, the deluded player is forever expecting too little or too much of himself and others. He suffers, because what he experiences is at odds with what he thinks he should experience. Often, he prowls the course feverishly, though unwittingly, seeking relief from himself.

In contrast to the deluded golfer, the wise golfer does what he can and accepts the results. He knows that there are good and bad days on the course. There are days when he has it and days when he does not. There are days when poor rounds turn good (and vice versa) and times when one falls into a trough of mediocrity. There are days and even entire seasons when the player is awake to the game, and times when the game loses its taste. The wise golfer knows that this is the way it is with golf, just as it is with life's other human endeavors.

The wise golfer understands defeat. He acknowledges that the game requires defeat, for without it, the game could not stimulate him, as only a false game would exclude defeat and its pain.

The mature golfer must have patience with himself and learn to trust his own efforts. He must even be willing to accept the fact that his devotion and sacrifice will not be rewarded with significant improvement. While seeking to improve, the player needs to recognize that on occasion he will have to sacrifice his game to the more serious demands of life.

He might approach the wisdom that Jerome Travis and James Crowell offered in *The Fifth Estate:*

> *The greatest pleasure derived from golf comes to those who have learned to play with a reasonable amount of accuracy. The happiest member of the golf family . . . is the fellow who consistently enjoys going around in the eighties and occasionally enjoys a round in the seventies. His game is good enough to steer him away from a frequency of dubbed shots. . . . Free of the troubles of the duffer, he has the bulge on the other extreme of the tribe, the seventy men, because he suffers no illusions about the bigger stakes of the sport and doesn't bother going in pursuit of them. It doesn't become a terrible calamity with him if he suddenly develops a slice from the tee or if his putts fail to behave as they should.*

It is impossible to tell a player with what wisdom he should approach the game. The elements that define a player's relation to the game belong to realms that exceed instruction and will. They postulate his having a wisdom that is as elusive as the insight upon which it rests.

A golfer plays his game the way he lives his life. If he matures in wisdom, he becomes aware of how much he has been given in life and learns to be grateful for it. He comes to understand his own desires and limits. He learns to take proper measure of himself in relation to others. At the same time, he takes care not to lose himself and his game in the mirror of others. He knows that feelings of jealousy, envy, arrogance, or superiority do not improve his play or increase his pleasure.

At every stage, even across mid-life, the golfer must make some efforts to improve his game, or at least stop it from deteriorating too badly. The good player cannot resign himself to bad shots any more than a good chess player could accept

making bad moves. The player is required to practice, and if
he is not blessed by the ability to enjoy practice, the game
costs him a lot in painful effort. At the same time, he must be
aware that efforts to improve his game, once he has reached a
high level, are rarely rewarded by significantly improved play.

As there must be a rhythm to his swing, so there must be a
pace to his game and a gate to its development. Over seasons,
he must treat the game as an old friend. He must keep an
equilibrium in his pursuit of the game, expecting neither too
much nor too little from it. There is nothing wrong with leaving golf for a season or two, or even much longer. In all likelihood (perhaps not with the speed of old friendships that are
rekindled by a single glance or word), the good player, especially one who learned the game in his youth when the swing
becomes a native language of the body, will not only reassem-
ble himself after a week's practice, but will have pleasures restored afresh for him after a vacation from the game.

The pleasures derived from the game finally depend on self-
knowledge. There is little likelihood that the golfer, no matter
how many books he reads or lessons he takes, will achieve the
wisdom required to properly enjoy the game. If the player
comes to the course confused about himself and the game,
what chance does he have to enjoy a round of golf in the company of his fellow golfers? If he approaches the game wanting
too little or too much from it, the game's pleasures will elude
him.

The wisdom praised here is simple. Even though it is not
directly attained or even perfectly embodied, it can be easily
stated without mystification: The wise golfer, knowing his
place in life and the game's place in the order of things, has the
key to its pleasures. Conversely, the deluded player, chained
to deceptions and illusions of his own making, suffers the
pain of being at odds with himself and the order of things.

At the heart of this wisdom, there is a recognition that golf is a game. It is contrived, artificial, and, most of all, superficial, but not superficial in the bad sense of the word. Golf is light and free. It belongs to the realm of play and poetry. It is *for* sight, sound, swing—and the hope for and the surprise of the unexpected.

Heavy-handed thinkers can choose to make golf a metaphor for life. They can suggest that a round of golf is somehow equivalent to living a life. It reveals the depths of an individual, testing the dimensions of his character. Yet for me, golf is like other sports and recreations. It should not be mystified to serve the author's vanity or to exclude the majority from its inner temple. Golf is about the pleasures of play.

The mysteries of golf are many. They are associated with what pleases the player and are about the nature of aim and the wonder of flight. They lead us to ask about the good swing, the wonderful shot, and the character of the great player. They turn around the ability of the player to practice and quit practicing, to remember and forget, to take the game seriously and not to take it seriously. But mysteries such as these do not merit mystification.

Though one half of golf is hidden within the player, the other half is manifest for the world to see. It is about being in the open, out in the wind, among friends, and under the skies. The player hits his ball through space, over and through obstacles, toward a series of small holes marked by flags. Golf is a circuitous and intriguing trail, a journey that has no destination other than the player's delight, no guidebook other than the rules of the game. The game exists because its players wish it to be.

The game also fits human nature. Man is a player (*Homo Ludens*), according to Dutch cultural historian, Johan Huizinga. Man sets up rules and plays by them. He defines limits and finds meaning by staying within them. He stipulates the significance of his actions. And in doing this, which goes to the essence of culture, he creates play. The game's play requires respect for its contrived nature. As this century shows well, when man stops playing and gets serious, he becomes dangerous.

Golf is a ritual. It is about participation and repetition. One plays and tallies, plays and tallies again. There is a familiarity of forms one follows from tee to green. Golf's primary sacrament suggests a connection between earth and heaven. The player participates in the grace of aiming and giving flight to an object. The sacrament joins body and mind, thought and motion, aim and target.

However, too much talk about golf's transcendence denies its simple earthly quality. Golf is a modest affair. After all, the golfer goes to the course, tees up his ball, and announces a fresh game. He walks, swings, and writes down his score on the hole. Golf provides an adventure without risk. It tests character without really probing its depths. Little or nothing turns on the outcome of play. The golfer leaves the course for the obligations and more important experiences of one's life.

By accepting the rules of the game, the player miniaturizes the world. Like the child at play, the golfer creates space and time for his game. And the game's keenest pleasures derive from the player's illusion that his little invented world of golf really matters. There he invests his attention and earnestness. He removes himself from the everyday realities of work and family. He is free of the jumble of feelings, sentiments, duties, and abstractions associated with family, work, and society. In contrast to the emotional, intellectual, and moral complexities of everyday life, play on the links provides sensual experience, emotional satisfaction, and calculable scores, readjustable in subsequent memories and conversations.

One outstanding player at our course, a nurse, took the game up seriously in her middle forties when her children were raised. She spent two years straight at the practice range. "Balls," she said, "are moved about easily, unlike children and sick people. They don't hurt and bleed. You swing, they fly, and you count. There is something refreshingly clean about this game." While she was never club champion, she became a good player.

The pleasure of every player is tied to the ability to put himself, if only momentarily, out of reach of the world. One early Sunday morning golfer at our country club who had a distinctly Irish name, when asked the question, "Are you missing Sunday mass again?" replied by tapping his driver three times on the tee and saying, "This is my mass. This is my mass. This is my mass." Then he whaled away at the ball as hard as he could. The other players so enjoyed this that the question and his reply became the initiating ritual of their Sunday round.

Another reason why the older player can love the game is because of the community it offers. Golf joins him not just to the fellow players he meets at the course, but to all those living and dead, who have known the ecstasy found in effortlessly launching a well-conceived shot along its envisioned path.

And, when the golfer tires of talk—even such high and mighty talk as this—he need only pick up his bag and head for the course. A fair wind is blowing, and there's a round to be played.

"With the increasing systemization and regimentation of sport, something of the pure play quality is inevitably lost."
—*Johan Huizinga,* **Homo Ludens**

"The culmination of the lawn culture of the nineteenth century was the establishment of twentieth-century country clubs and golf courses, the suburban equivalent of the urban park."
—*Virginia Jenkins,*
The Lawn—A History of an American Obsession

CONCLUSION

Return to the Caddie House

I RETURNED TO THE COUNTRY CLUB forty years after I had started working there as a boy of twelve, and discovered that the royal and ancient game of golf had changed as much as I had in the intervening decades.

On the way out to the course on that bright Fall day, I observed how the properties of Grosse Pointe Woods, many of which were carved out of the lake estates in the late 1950s and 1960s, had withstood the test of time. They stood in sharp contrast to my boyhood neighborhood on the east side of Detroit, which had changed drastically since expressway I-94 had sliced my neighborhood in two in 1955, burying my home beneath several lanes of concrete. I then moved with my family to the suburbs, where the earlier feeling of community was never recovered.

As I entered the country club's parking lot (I had returned only a handful of times since I left the club in the fall of 1956 for the University of Michigan), I felt I had reentered the garden of my youth. I was struck by how things had remained the same: the secluded drive-in, the ample parking lot, and the English country home–style clubhouse. The same black and blue slate roofs dominated the landscape, which was defined by carefully manicured shrubs and trees. However, the paddleball courts that had been tucked in along the south side of the clubhouse were now gone. Out of the corner of my eye, I saw a foursome on the first tee. In my mind, I pictured myself there bending my own tee shot with a slight running draw hook, evading the rough and the large, deep, circular bunker at about 245 yards out on the right, and bringing the ball into the right center of the fairway. From there, the well-trapped and long but narrow green opened to an eight or nine iron.

Upon entering the foyer of the clubhouse, which I had only momentarily done a handful of times as a caddie, I felt time had been frozen, and for an instant, I was almost envious, as the club's members had maintained a continuity in life that had evaded me.

Lunch with Mr. Standish

A black receptionist greeted me. I remembered that when important members hosted coming-out parties for their daughters at the club, uniformed blacks greeted long rows of guests in their cars as they arrived. The high timbered ceiling, crisscrossed with rafters, and the shining tile floor still impressed me. Everything was impeccably clean. I identified myself and explained that Mr. John Standish had invited me for lunch.

Mr. Standish, president of Michigan Golf Association and a bank vice president, was an outstanding golfer himself. His father was one of the club's all-time best golfers, a four-time winner of the Michigan Amateur between 1909 and 1924, and president of the United States Golf Association for two years in the early 1950s, just previous to our club hosting the 1954 National Amateur Championship. Mr. Standish arrived on time and led me to the grill for lunch and a short chat about the history of the club. As we entered the grill, he pointed to the wall where there hung a Herbert Wind article from *Sports Illustrated* that featured Palmer and Sweeny's duel for that 1954 National Amateur. The article described the long, grueling test between the graceful and aged Englishman, Robert Sweeny, and the youthful and determined American, Arnold Palmer, who wore a bleached red baseball cap throughout the tournament. The article featured a photograph in which appeared my closest boyhood friend, Ron Helveston, who was Sweeny's caddie. Standing as he often did with his hand on his hip and his elbow out, Ron watched Sweeny's attempt to recover from a seriously pushed tee shot on the thirty-sixth and final hole of the tournament. Palmer's victory there catapulted him into the national limelight.

During my conversation with John, I inquired about old members. I found it strange—and in a way, he must have, too—that in this conversation caddie and member had somehow been made equal, as the passage of time had made us part of the same family portrait. Distances between player and caddie were now spanned by common memories.

John explained why there have been no major tournaments at the club since the '54 Amateur: The course isn't equipped for such crowds, nor are its members desirous of such ballyhoo. They have their club; it has its history; they and their community don't need the world's glory. I found myself cheering for this "old aristocratic" resistance to the ways of the new business class. I thought how noble was that house-owner at the entrance of the Royal Birkdale who declined hundreds of thousands of dollars to have the circular front of his house painted as a Coca Cola can during a recent British Open. Perhaps it is money that permits such principles. Nevertheless, the club's refusal to hold tournaments rings sweet when compared to the nearly uninterrupted clatter of golf professionals and merchandisers selling anything and everything they can in the name of the game. As golf previously carried with it the shame (at least in certain political and cultural circles) of being a rich man's game, it now has the added shame—a kind of prostitution of sorts—of seeing its best players turn their extraordinary blessings into enormous commercial opportunities.

When lunch was finished, Mr. Standish led me out of the grill and down to the spot at the back of the eighteenth hole where Palmer's recovery chip won him the Amateur. Many years later, the members had put a small marble marker where Palmer struck that winning shot. Palmer, playing nearby at the time, flew in by helicopter to attend the inauguration of the spot. A similar marker exists next to a small tree on the fifteenth hole of the Royal Birkdale where, in the 1961 British Open, Palmer struck, from what most took to be an absolutely unplayable lie in the scrub, an extraordinary one-hundred-and-forty-yard shot onto the elevated green, thus assuring him victory. Like battlefield monuments, these markers help define the official historical memory of golf's great shots and turning points for the handful of players who find pleasure in the history of the game.

The Vanished Old Hole

Mr. Standish then escorted me to the first tee, where he introduced me to the twosome teeing off and to the club professional. Feeling like a graybeard who had been put on the stage to say a thing or two about the past, I did my duty. I mentioned a few of the old professionals and told them about the old hole, which bespoke an era before these youngster's time. Mr. Standish then introduced me to the caddie-master and explained that he and the club's members were doing what they could to restore and preserve caddies with a new program. It made me feel as if I was hearing a botanist describe his work to save an endangered species.

In place of the short, thick, and powerful Caesar Raimondi who ran the caddie shack in my day, stood a quiet, gentle young man. He didn't refer to himself as a caddie-master (after all, who could call himself a master of anyone in this era?). Rather, he described himself as—I believe—a golf resource manager. In addition to getting caddies (of which fewer are needed these days), he also furnished carts to the members. As part of the program to encourage members to take caddies (and also for aesthetic reasons), only a few golf carts were seen at the first tee.

Caddies now earned substantial fees, the manager explained—$15 for 18 holes, compared to $2.50 tops in my days. He said that he had a little difficulty finding caddies, who were now from the middle class—precisely from a class likely to hire caddies themselves on occasions. However, the improvement in rates (not that great when inflation is considered) did not spell a corresponding improvement in the caddie shed itself. Inside the caddie house, the decline of the caddie's place in the game was palpable. The 25-foot by 15-foot room in which the caddies waited had not been painted for a long time. On the same cement floor sat the same long, blond-colored, slatted benches on which I had sat four decades earlier waiting for a loop or killing time on a rainy day. The benches on one side of the shed had been shortened, so there was room for three large video games. I wondered whether today's caddies spent spare time chatting and playing cards as we did.

The video game in the shed expressed for me the contemporary mind's preference for pleasure based on sight, speed, and instant gratification. This immediacy stands in sharp contrast to the traditional world, whose leisures were attached to slower rhythms of walking and talking. Indeed, little more than a century ago, except in the tapping hands of the new telegraphers, electricity did not yet drive machines or dictate the pulse of contemporary power and pleasure. Planes had not yet taken flight. The world at that time was slower and less colorful. Early golf paintings from that period reveal groups of heavily-clad men and even more heavily-clad women who went in great groups out of the clubhouse to observe long rivalries with one another as they paraded in procession from hole to hole.

The back door of the caddie shed was blocked and the caddies no longer had access to the space out back where we had spent our free time between loops. They had lost access to the open areas where, under the canopy of small scotch pines, we idled away our time, chipping between trees, sitting at one of the few picnic tables trying out our wisecracking, or playing horseshoes, dominated by pro Ray Milan with his ability to throw a flat shoe that opened after a three-quarter turn on its way to the stake.

It struck me as even more revelatory of the caddie's diminished place in the game that caddies no longer had a place to practice golf and couldn't sit on the edge of the driving range and observe. The driving range was the place, at least in my day, where a caddie might pick up a few tips from one of the assistants, and where on his way down to the old hole he could pocket a ball or two for play. The old hole, where my friend Ron and I took our first turns at the game, no longer existed. The old hole and other open adjacent land on the southeast corner of the course had been sacrificed to a new three-hole executive course intended for quicker play.

At the country club, the caddies' place in the game was diminished, as it has been everywhere else in the game except on the pro tour. On the pro tour, the caddie has increasingly emerged as a full-time professional who works for a salary and percentage of his player's earnings. However, the caddies' traditional claim to be numbered among the game's best players has all but disappeared. Caddies, who dominated the ranks of the professionals from the era of Ouimet and Sarazen through the age of Nelson and Hogan (the last great caddie players), no longer supply the game with its great players, and they no longer add significantly to the game's color. Caddies have become, so to speak, a walking anachronism. They have gone the way of a lot of other old breeds, such as household servants, craftsmen, and even peasants like my grandparents from Sicily. Groups such as these perished at the hands of a world mechanized, standardized, and organized for more and faster pleasures.

The Cart & the Carpet

The golf cart, more than anything else, has caused (even symbolized) the caddies' demise. The golf cart marks the end of walking on the course and mirrors modern life in general. How much less we all walk! How much more we sit and how much more modern work is about sitting rather than walking. (Truly there should be, if there already is not, a history about the curtailment of walking in our world.) The cart has become the new servant of the golfer in this servantless age. And even when most discretely introduced, as it was at our country club (fleets of them hidden away behind the pro shop), the cart is still an interloper in the garden. It brings a new realm of sounds, not just the zooming, whining, and the squeaking brakes of the machine plus the clattering of clubs, but people even have carts with TVs and radios so they can monitor other sporting events while they golf.

The cart also redefines the space of the golf course. Slow players are made fast; foursomes with carts press twosomes that walk; and individual players with carts zoom in all directions to meet friends or retrieve their forgotten clubs. Then, too, it brings new senses of sociability when you are forced to accommodate your play and enjoyment of the game to the player sharing your cart.

The cart also creates the new course, as the majority of new courses are designed around the obligation of players to ride in a cart. On many courses, players are not even allowed to walk. Furthermore, carts introduce bands of concrete all over the course, and produce a whole new set of lucky and ugly shots. Nothing is as hideous to a golfer as the sound and sight of a golf ball bouncing on cement or asphalt, regardless of where it ends up. Carts also wear down the roughs on dry and sandy courses, destroying the grass itself and leaving one of the least possible shots in golf: a high lofted pitch off hard, deadpan ground.

Worse yet is how the cart changes the feel of the game. It makes golf a drive-and-shoot affair. Universal adoption of yardage markers has also furthered drive-and-shoot target golf. Yardage markers gained popularity in the 1960s and 1970s with the planting of 150-yard tree markers along the edge of the fairway. By the 1980s more and more courses introduced blue, white, and red disks in the fairway, respectively marking 200-, 150-, and 100-yard distances from the green. Some clubs, like my own, have recently introduced electronic pins which permit a properly equipped player to determine his exact distance from the pin. Of course, the desire of members for exact yardage imitates the professional's long-standing concern for establishing exact yardage. The concept is right club, right swing, right shot.

This golf of know-the-distance, hit-the-shot can only thrive when flight, not roll, primarily determines a shot's outcome. This form of target golf depends on a course design that features the regular mowing and watering of the course, tasks that depend on new technologies. Greenskeepers, now known as course superintendents, have spent three decades transforming formerly dry, barren, irregular courses with coarse fairways and infrequently-mowed greens into "little Augustas."

Contemporary players of the game demand a different kind of golf. A retired greenskeeper from a Minneapolis country club once confided to me of his picky members: "They want to play golf in the Garden of Eden. They won't accept the rub of the green anymore. Every damn bounce must be perfect." He castigated golfers who, like the professionals molding their ideals for the game, are against adversity in all but the most predictable forms. "They've seen too much TV. They want the course to be perfect at all times. Christ!" he blurted out in exasperation, "They only want to play on bent!"

It was hard to disagree with him. As early as the 1890s, commentators on the game described the desire of some golfers to make their greens as smooth as billiard tables. Today even members of the smallest, poorest, and most out-of-the-way clubs now seek to turn their greens into carpets and make their fairways better than any lawn. They engineer their course's slopes, deflect its brooks and streams, build ponds, and select, tailor, and regulate its vegetation as closely as a gardener monitors his garden. They irrigate the course as much as possible. They spray on all the herbicide legally allowed, selecting a preferred grass and obliterating all others. Nothing but near-perfect fairways and greens satisfy them.

They insist that greenskeepers—keepers of the green—have perfect control of earth and water. And, as in all things, the greenskeepers—course superintendents—specialize in new sciences and technologies. Greenskeepers once learned their craft in apprenticeship on a nearby farm at the course, but are now educated in special college programs. Like any college student, they take a whole range of horticultural, botanical, and golf course management classes. Computers and science, seminars and professional magazines are all part of the greenskeepers' trade.

The greenskeeper has increasingly become the object of the passions golfers formerly reserved for "the rub of the green." Like the modern doctor, the greenskeeper is expected to cure all and is the target of growing blame. "Every course should be as perfect as Augusta," is the new imperative. Members insist on perfection. They call their greenskeepers to ever higher standards and even want them to beautify their courses with flowers and trees, as if golf courses were flower gardens. Parks and lawns were once used exclusively by the residents of the dwellings of royalty and the high aristocracy, but they are now the playing fields of the majority. Excess money and leisure time, combined with technologies to mold the earth, water, and grasses, have allowed everyone to dream of pleasures unspoiled by imperfection. Even the winds are viewed by some as a deterrent to a perfect round in golf's modern garden.

A Visit with a Greenskeeper

After visiting the caddie house, I drove out onto the course to see some of its wonderful interior holes and to visit the club's greenskeeper. A graduate of Michigan State's golf course program and an ardent golfer himself, he was quick to confirm the diagnosis that players wanted flawless courses by examples from the country club itself. Without mentioning names, he said members were increasingly averse to the rub of the green. They also coveted a perfect lawn and, from the oldest to the youngest to the weakest, wanted a course that every player could play with some success, a demand that meant wide-open fairways and short, thin roughs.

He told me that members started a wonderful tree replanting program in response to the devastation wrought on the course by Dutch Elm disease. They planted hundreds of trees of over a hundred varieties, which naturally added to his work. The list of trees, which he printed out from his computer, included not only an array of common trees, but such exotic trees as Amur Cork, Ginko, Crimean Linden, and Siberian Spruce. Furthermore, he explained, the tree planting program had developed a life of its own. While enthusiastic members sought to plant yet more trees, certain members had to resist the noble (but misguided and encroaching) impulse of other members to turn the course into an arboretum. Trees, they needed to be told, don't always improve a course.

As I listened to the greenskeeper talk, the course, frozen in time by my nostalgia, began to melt. The course was not independent from society's growing control of water, soil, and plants. Rather, its fate followed society's powers to transform deserts, prairies, marshes, streams, rivers, and lakes. The contemporary golf course truly belongs to the history of contemporary agriculture, gardens, and lawns.

A single painful thought bounced back and forth in my head: The golf course was as artificial as the video games that the new generation of caddies played. The golf course itself, I concluded, belongs to the world of man-made things; it is one of the most artificial of human creations. To a greater extent than even the cemetery, the course is the lawn of lawns, the garden of gardens. Its grass, trees, and grounds have been shaped to the game. This country club—my youthful garden—was not the antithesis of, but the creation of, the rich, powerful, industrial city, Detroit.

New Power, New Fun

No American example of the emerging power of modern civilization and its favorite recreation, golf, is as telling as the case of the building of Shinnecock Hills, an early course on Long Island. According to Herbert Warren Wind, William Vanderbilt (son of American railway magnate Cornelius Vanderbilt), and a few friends invited Scottish pro Willie Dunn to build a course for "a fitting sport for the nation." In 1891, Dunn transformed 4,000 acres along Great Peconic Bay into a twelve-hole golf course. Wind writes: "With a crew of 150 Indians from the nearby Shinnecock reservation and a few horse-drawn road scrapers, Dunn cleared the fairways, removed the blueberry bushes from the rough and, not afraid of bringing down a curse on the course, utilized the Indian burial mounds as obstacles before the greens or made them into sandtraps." The dead here were not allowed to stand in the way of the living. Rather, they were used to serve the pleasures of the living.

In 1900 (just ten years after Dunn turned the burial mounds of Shinnecock into bunkers and the same year the great British professional, Harry Vardon, made his tour of America) the game, according to Wind, "had established itself as more than the coddled crush of the gilded set—something more than racquets or squash tennis." It was seen as a recreation open to both sexes. Its leading missionaries were the upper-class college set, who found in the game a way to wear "dashing outfits" and spend a good slice of their income. In

1900, the nation already had a thousand courses and was spending millions of dollars a year to play the game. There was at least one course in every state, with New York and Massachusetts leading the way with 165 and 157 respectively. Chicago created its municipal course, Jackson Park, by filling in a field with the bricks, concrete pillars, and other debris from the 1893 World's Fair. Progress literally provided the basis for golf.

Golf's popularity, which began in the second half of the preceding century with the upper-merchant classes, is tied to the spread of wealth and leisure. In the first half of this century, it reached the whole middle class. It reached the working class in the English speaking world in the second half of this century. In the last hundred and fifty years, golf's dramatic spread from Scotland to the British Isles, and from Britain to the United States, Canada, Australia, New Zealand, Europe, and to the non-English speaking world, reveals golf's inseparable relation to the world-wide growth of commercial and industrial society.

The transformation of the golf course from a provisional layout on rough and marginal lands to a pleasing garden, is integral to advancing civilization's control over nature and a society's desire of distracting comforts. One hundred and fifty years ago, golfers played the game where they could. They contended with giant dunes, undulating moguls, immense stretches of rough, thickets of gorse, fields of heather and rushes, wet grounds and marshlands, drainage ditches and channels, as well as with grazing animals (especially where courses were laid out on common grounds), rabbit warrens, walls, railroad lines, telegraph poles, roads, and ruts. Indeed, wetlands explain the earlier popularity of the water iron—a club with a rake-like head or having a head with holes bored through it, while wagon ruts accounted for the creation of an exceptionally small-headed iron called the rut iron. All of the impediments singularly and in juxtaposition gave early courses a distinct charm, though they were composed of peculiar terrors, great surprises, and offered the pleasures of making Odysseus-like recovery shots.

Avid nineteenth-century Scottish golf enthusiasts created courses as economically as they could. They rented or purchased inexpensive wastelands (some of which were known as muirs, hence Muirfield) for a few pounds. With minimal alteration of the terrain, they laid out courses of six and nine holes. In the case of St. Andrews, which established the eighteen-hole standard, its economies included using seven of the same greens (though considerably enlarged) for both outgoing play on the front nine and incoming play on the back nine. At the Royal Liverpool, located at the seaside suburb of Hoylake, members turned the inner circle of a race track into a small course. Prestwick, a seaside course in western Scotland, was founded in 1851 and became host to the first British Open in 1860. There players encountered, as they still do as part of its historical charm, crossing fairways, tees directly behind greens, a railroad track forming out-of-bounds on the terrifyingly short beginning hole, par fours that the boldest can reach with one stroke and par fours that no one can reach in two against prevailing winds when they blow strong, and even two blind greens, which require golfers to ring giant gongs to signal their departure from the green. The Royal North Devon, the first seaside links course in England (established by Scots), reveals its origin as a common ground, as it is still covered with grazing sheep. Aside from filling fairways and bedding down in sand traps, the sheep, which leave the low-mowed greens alone, do their part by trimming and fertilizing the course's fairways. The club secretary told me a small sum is paid out annually for dead sheep, whose owners claim they were killed on the course.

In contrast to these original courses, which often underwent fifty years of willy-nilly development before taking form as now-standard eighteen-hole courses, contemporary courses are constructed at dizzying speeds, in stunning numbers, on the drafting boards of remote international golf architectural firms. In keeping with the strengths of modern civilization, contemporary architects transform earth and waters, and alter and import vegetation. They dynamite and bulldoze the earth; fill, pack, mound, and pile up dirt behind railroad ties; change the soils, and grow new and foreign grasses. In turn, they drain water, channel streams, and create ponds and lakes. They even create island greens that can be moved mechanically. Their artificially-engineered gardens are more refined and tamer than their predecessors.

Approximately 200 new golf courses a year are built in the United States. Hundreds more are built in Europe and Asia, adding to the world's 21,000 courses. Cumulatively, they serve as leisure communities for retirees, vacationers, and resorters alike. They involve property transactions, land development, and commercial and civic boosterism. They have profound social and ecological consequences: Wet and dry lands, prairie and woodlands, flat and hilly lands cannot be molded into greens and fairways without altering terrains, changing water tables, and eliminating native plants and animals.

New Gods, New Courses

Golf increasingly conforms to the gods of money, numbers, and speed, the ruling deities that become the real architects of the new courses. Offering straight-forward pleasures, they banish the luck, disaster, and disgrace that made golf on the old links resemble life in the older order. These new courses carry the names of such prestigious players as Nicklaus,

Palmer, and Weiskopf, and offer the pleasure of playing a championship course. The courses, as expected, copy, adopt, and steal holes and names from classic links courses.

As courses change, so do the pleasures of the game. In its contemporary form, golf (at least for the majority) is about driving and shooting. Left behind is the rhythm of the older world. The pace of the new game resembles the stop-and-go urgency of contemporary urban life. Players formerly walked around a course as if part of a slower and more solemn procession. They went from tee to green and from green to tee as if they were a special entourage. They left the teeing area together and soon separated, played their own shots, and rejoined. They stopped occasionally as they entered upon long, circling searches for lost balls, or as they huddled in shared consideration of lengthy chips and putts.

Golf today is entirely different. The processional and ceremonial quality of the game is gone. Foursomes (and even fivesomes) are squeezed off tees and along fairways like parts on an assembly line. The course is traversed by erratically accelerating carts and resembles a factory of jerking mechanical stops and starts. At the busiest times, courses resemble those busy lakes where boats with waterskiers and jet skiers noisily charge back and forth. Indeed, how could it be otherwise—golf belongs to a civilization that tames and shrinks the world and hastily grasps for its pleasures.

The Kingdom of Golfdom

As golf was once exclusive, local, and improvised, so the new game, yielding to new and superior forces, is standardized. Local clubs lose their autonomy and sense of community as their players, whose games once focused around their home club, now conceive of golf as belonging to a national and even to an international community.

To a large degree, golf and its pleasures have already become a set of manipulated images. A larger and larger portion of the game is experienced on television by an ever greater number of its enthusiasts. At the same time, golf is transformed into video and computer games. Indeed, virtual reality has already become golf reality. Players simulate playing great courses at their local indoor-driving ranges, or by clicking the mouse on their home computer.

Golf media also lives off and nurtures the mass and commercial cultures that increasingly envelop the game, furnishing portraits of great players overshadowing the play of all others. Television offers the standard images and styles of play, and defines the pains and pleasures of the game.

Local golf has been sacrificed to mass, national, and abstract golf, and is increasingly overrun by distant interests, agencies, and images. At the same time, golfers' pleasures are confined to ever more regulated gardens, whose adventures and risks are engineered to profit. The standardization of equipment, swing, course, and style of play are no different. As unpleasant as this thought is, it must in measure be conceded that golf is merely another of society's commercially-defined grooves intended to absorb our extra time and money. Golf is like everything else that has matured in the last century, as our pacts with the devil have involved attaining power and happiness at the price of more money, greater numbers, and quicker pleasures.

Golf professionals and their associations support the homogenization of the game, and they are the acting sheriffs of the kingdom of golfdom. Standing at the nexus between local play and national control and profits, the professionals bring the new rules and regulations and recent fashions to their home courses. While professionals play the local role of "swing therapist," merchandiser, tournament organizer, and even reconciler between factions, they also serve as on-site mentors of the national game, promoting its new orthodoxies, mass commodities, and fashions.

Professional players (as has been easily observable since the 1920s) belong to the recreation and entertainment industries. Those at the very top profit handsomely. Others can work their way into clubs or teach at driving ranges or sell golf merchandise. As in the case of other sports, the increasingly common path to a career in golf is collegiate golf. In college tournaments, the aspirant can take further measure of himself and his peers to see whether the risk of another four to ten years of his life invested in a game is worthwhile.

Jack Nicklaus, winner of 55 PGA tour victories, five PGA championships, six Masters tournaments, four U.S. Opens, and three British Opens, indisputably the most heralded player of recent times, shows the nexus between golfing talent and money-making ability. In Nicklaus's case, a business career blossomed simultaneously with his professional golfing career, beginning in 1961. Far from the fairways and greens that he knew so well, Nicklaus tried his hand at business and lost, according to Glen Waggoner's *The Greening of the Golden Bear,* a sizable $21 million in cash. Golden Bear International was built on real estate development, a Pontiac dealership, a shrimp farm, a financial services company, a radio station, a travel agency, an oil- and gas-exploration partnership, and dozens of endorsement and licensing deals. By the mid-1980s, Nicklaus and his company "teetered on the edge of insolvency." Nicklaus's sixth Masters victory was in 1986, and business reorganization of Golden Bear came just in time to save Jack and his company. Jack's revived kingdom, still based on golf and on his golfing name, now includes his endorsements of a host of products (from insulations to telephones), a golf school, golf communities, television videos, fifteen books and $3.5 million in sales, a sports agency, the

Memorial Tournament, golf clubs, and, above all else, golf course design. Waggoner lists 93 courses bearing Nicklaus's name in the world. "Nicklaus's design fees—$1.25 million in the U.S.A. and Europe, $1.5 million in Asia, $2.1 in Japan—are the industry's highest by a significant margin. As the course design business goes," Waggoner concludes, "so goes Golden Bear International." Jack Nicklaus is certainly not alone in the annals of modern sport to try to turn his blessings in the game into commercial good fortune.

Golf and its players are like most other products of industrial society. With so many people playing golf, how could there not be some who play it wonderfully? Millions of players swing; hundreds of thousands play seriously; tens of thousands develop good games; thousands become outstanding; and of those, hundreds and hundreds become recognized, if only for a season or two. It is no wonder there are so many great golfers and great rounds of golf. From a certain point of view, great players—even a Nicklaus—are not wonders. Rather, they are likely statistical outcomes. If so many people play roulette so many times, it is not surprising—at least statistically—that one color will come up twenty-six times in a row, as black did in Monte Carlo on August 18, 1923. If so many professional players hit baseballs, it is not unexpected that one of them would hit in 56 straight games as Joe DiMaggio did in 1941. The games of the professionals themselves, however wonderful they may be, have, accordingly, become more statistically predictable and ultimately boring like the mass society that gave them birth.

Preserving a Friendship

The player who wishes to preserve his friendship with the game will have to struggle to keep his relations with it personal. He will have to fight to protect his pleasure in the game from degradation by many contemporary vices associated with its popularity, commerce, and regulation. At the same time, like the monks of old fighting sin, he must recognize that the game's core pleasures can be lost to pride, vanity, greed, anger, and other vices.

As in any friendship, the golfer who wishes to keep the game a matter of abiding pleasures must stay keen of mind and accept the notion that his relationship with golf changes, just as his mind and body changes. His pleasures may not be as sharp and poignant as he ages, but they may be fuller and more gentle. As prescribed by the old Epicurean philosopher in his garden, with care and thought the golfer's pleasures can rest more on the appreciation of the play of others, and also on the quiet, peace, and friendship that the game sustains.

The player who wishes to sustain his golfing pleasures does well if he mixes them. A variety of pleasures derived from the game is more likely to endure than is a single pleasure, however intense. Pleasures are to be had in reading the history of golf, in collecting old clubs, in writing a history of one's own club, in understanding what the greenskeeper does, or in aiding in the course's redesign. An occasional moderate bet, a trip to other courses, improvising different tees for existing holes, or organizing tournaments with a single club are all things that might variegate and increase his pleasure.

There are other simple things a player can do to preserve the pleasures of the game. He can abandon his cart. He can take more interest in local stories and play of the game. He can play a round or two with clubs of a different era, so that he can feel the different torque of the shafts and the touch of the blades and come to appreciate the shotmaking from earlier times. Also, he can seek out more primitive courses—I would especially recommend seaside links—where course conditions, recovery shots, invented shots, running shots, approach shots, blind shots, and luck itself play a far larger role than they do on today's target golf courses.

If I were allowed to follow my own fanciful bent, I would have a handful of committed golfers form clubs open only to walking golfers, with a minimal clubhouse, where play would be on modestly-kept fairways bordered by far wilder roughs of mixed grasses and plants. The demons and deviltry of golf's origins would be restored to these courses and the "rub of the green" would again be an accepted condition of play. And the wind would be up as much as possible.

Until such a time as the golfer finds his way on to such renegade courses, he would do well to seek the more rural and isolated courses, and make himself into a bad weather player, an early Spring and late Fall player—even a Winter golfer— when he will find the course empty and his own. Then he can have not only the pleasure of playing at his own pace, but can even, if the course is wide open, invent his own holes. Alone, or in the company of a few good golfing companions, one can engage in the wonder of playing golf one's own way.

Playing the game somewhere between sheer earnestness and utter frivolity, the golfer can momentarily lend himself to the illusion that what he does with ball and club on this little patch of earth somehow matters. He can have a reason to be walking out in the wind. He can delight in the grace of the effortless swing and enjoy the sight of a ball set aflight on course. He can gratefully accept the grace of the God who lets us—we who are not quite angels—play so fervently in a garden where mind and matter occasionally coincide.

AFTERWORD

Leon Rappoport

I FEEL RATHER UNIQUELY QUALIFIED to comment on Joe Amato's discourse on his life in golf because I know nothing at all about golf, never attempted to play, and always wondered why anyone would want to watch such a slow, tedious, so-called "sport." As a form of enjoyable activity, for me golf ranked somewhere between solving math problems and learning Latin. Consequently, if *I* can find his meditations on golf to be fascinating, I'm sure many others will. Perhaps that is enough said, but let me elaborate.

Most of us more or less spontaneously acquire our preferences for sports and games somewhere between the ages of 10 and 16. Part of it, of course, is simply a matter of exposure, yet from among the various activities we first experience, some begin to stand out as particularly attractive because they

---

Dr. Leon Rappoport is professor of psychology at Kansas State University. He is the author of many books, including *Zen and the Art of Running, The Holocaust and the Crisis of Human Behavior, Personality Development, History of Aggression,* and *Varieties of Psychohistory.*

seem to resonate with our mind-body "type" or "being." For Joe, as he tells us, it was golf: his first experience at age 12 of working as a caddie at the Detroit Country Club. And it must have been something like love at first sight, because he quickly developed an intuitive sense of connection not only with the physical challenge of the sport, but the deeper aesthetic, mental and social aspects as well; those things that have stayed with him all his life and are described so lyrically in this book.

In my case, however, at about age 12 it was football. I was a tall, skinny, fast runner with quick reaction times who loved the scuffle and hustle of going deep for a long pass. Unlike golf, this was not something that required much in the way of thought or patience. More to the point were fast moves and a large tolerance for scrapes and bruises. Not surprisingly, I later moved on to downhill skiing and, for the warm months, tennis. Given this background, it should be apparent why throughout most of my life I thought of golf as a game for slow moving sissies and rich country clubbers. It is all the more impressive to me, therefore, to finally see how wrong I have been. Joe Amato, you have lifted the scales from mine eyes! (At least so far as golf is concerned.)

What I have realized from reading this book is that although golf can be engaged simply as a game or sport with enjoyable possibilities open to persons of every age and level of skill, it is ultimately, and most profoundly, a pathway leading into embodied metaphysical experience. That is, the book is in many ways comparable to Herrigel's classic *Zen and the Art of Archery,* because starting with similarly straightforward physical tasks—shooting an arrow, hitting a golf ball—both reach out to encompass the same wide range of psychosocial and philosophical issues.

Fundamentally, the similarities between Amato's discussion of golf and Herrigel's work on zen archery center on the experience of unity or "oneness" between the person and the activity. Thus, Amato's detailed descriptions of the golfers total concentration on the heft and swing of the club, intake and control of the breath, the moment of contact with the ball, and the immediate sense of whether or not its flight will end in the target zone, is almost perfectly parallel to Herrigel's description of shooting an arrow. And Amato's discussion of the vagaries of golfing instruction manuals, the infinite lore concerning body postures, ways to achieve the perfect swing, or to correct one's imperfections, which have finally led him to conclude that most if not all of such self-improvement discourses are not very useful, is reminiscent of the ancient zen saying, "those who say do not know, those who know do not say."

In sum, and in countless other ways apart from those noted above, Amato provides such splendid insights into the metaphysics of golf that even a non-golfer like me can appreciate them. More specifically, what emerges from his narrative is the realization that while golf masquerades as a simple game—hitting a ball into a cup—it is in reality a challenge to master the unmasterable! That is, the game requires players to learn a seemingly endless repertoire of complex mind-body skills, each involving a unique configuration of cognitive and perceptual-motor variables. Hitting a pitched baseball, for example, is essentially one unitary act with a number of small variations, and a batter can always blame failure on the pitcher. The golfer's drive, putt, or chip shot, however, are each quite singular, in that skill at any one of them does not carry over to any other, and there is no way to disown responsibility for failure. Moreover, in addition to the different demands of each golfing task, they must be accomplished while taking into account the effect of ever-changing conditions: the wind, the lie of the ball, the contours of the course, etc. It is this complex variability and solitary nature of the sport that guarantees the unavoidable, exquisitely painful frustrations suffered by players (even world-class champions, as Amato eloquently points out) facing the ever-changing conditions of mind, body, weather, and terrain. Paradoxically, this is also the source of the wisdom of golf: the challenges of play that inevitably force the serious golfer into the metaphysics of internal dialogue and self-scrutiny.

Here, at the core of what has been trivialized by some writers as "the inner game of golf," is where Amato's reflections shade into the domains of transcendentalist philosophy. He makes no pretentions to the status of a Ralph Waldo Emerson, but the implicit theme is that just as the unexamined life is not worth living, the unexamined golf game is not worth playing. This is where he reveals what can be learned from a lifelong struggle to master the unmasterable challenges of getting the ball into the cup at par! And this is where readers may finally discover what it means to at last reach that state of harmony which lies at the far end of the struggle.

I have no way of knowing if veteran golfers will have enjoyed this book as much as I have. I should think they would. I do know that it has transformed my anti-golf prejudice into admiration. And if I could have Joe Amato as my instructor, I'd be ready to try it myself.

INDEX

About the Author

Joseph Amato is Director of Regional Studies and a professor of history at Southwest State University in Marshall, Minnesota. Professor Amato's is the author of fifteen books and many articles that reflect his dedication to and interest in European intellectual and cultural history as well as rural and regional history. These include *Mounier and Maritain: A French Catholic Understanding of the Modern World; Guilt and Gratitude: A Study of the Origins of Contemporary Conscience; Victims and Values: A History and A Theory of Suffering; The Great Jerusalem Artichoke Circus: The Buying and Selling of the Rural American Dream; Ethics, Living or Dead?; Death Book: Terrors, Consolations, Contradictions and Paradoxes; Countryside: Mirror of Ourselves; When Father and Son Conspire: A Minnesota Farm Murder; Servants of the Land;* and *A New College on the Prairie.*

This book was set into type
by Crossings Press
in 11/14 Stempel Garamond, a modern
adaptation by the Stempel foundry, Frankfurt,
of the classic French typeface
designed by Claude Garamond
in the 16th century.
Chapter headings are Castellar
& Stempel Garamond Bold Italic.

Cover: Printed on 10 pt. C1S Cornwall Coated Cover
Text: Printed on 60 lb. Smooth Cream Fusion Opaque